computers
&
systems

an introduction for librarians

computers & systems

an introduction for librarians

JOHN EYRE ALA & PETER TONKS MBCS

FIRST PUBLISHED 1971 BY CLIVE BINGLEY LTD
16 PEMBRIDGE ROAD LONDON W11
SET IN 10 ON 13 LINOTYPE PLANTIN AND
PRINTED IN GREAT BRITAIN BY THE CENTRAL PRESS (ABERDEEN) LTD

0 85157 120 4

contents

list of illustrations

introduction

The continual cry from those attending the data processing courses at the School of Librarianship of the Polytechnic of North London has been for a simple and uncomplicated book on computers. Such a work was to outline what a computer does, especially in the library context, and explain in general terms what systems work is about. After four years of running these courses for both non-graduates and graduates, we decided that the time had finally come to attempt to meet this need. At the risk of being charged with adding to an already prolific area of literature we have produced this book as an introduction specifically written for librarians or library students. Most works on computers seem to delve into the technicalities too deeply for the requirements of those wishing simply to know what are the potentials and limitations of a computer in the library. The other objection to many of the presently available books was that the accent was placed on commercial examples used to illustrate computer applications. These do not help much when the reader is thinking in terms of bibliographic records and information retrieval; areas quite outside commercial practice.

We are conscious of the excellent works which have been published on computers in libraries, but all these seem either to assume a knowledge of computer workings or are intended to instruct the reader on methodology. A selection of such works has been given in a bibliography at the end of this book so that those wishing to pursue the matter further can do so profitably. There are of course many periodical articles on the computer in the library, but these tend to give very individualised views of systems in the making and, though valuable, often defeat the uninitiated.

With all these points in mind, we have tried to cover the subject of the computer in a way which will be at once simple and informative. In order to keep the length of the book realistic in the light of its intended purpose we have had to simplify many aspects which might otherwise have required considerable technical detail to cover fully, and we have therefore contented ourselves with a presentation of what may be termed the overall view.

As may be expected, no work of this kind can be produced without help or encouragement from colleagues. It is appropriate to record our sincere thanks to them, and especially to Mr A Croghan of our teaching staff and Miss M Ritchie of our research staff for their invaluable criticisms and suggestions. Our sincere thanks must also go to the teaching staff of the School of Librarianship, for the farsighted support of our data processing courses which have now become a regular part of this school's curriculum.

April, 1971

JOHN EYRE
PETER TONKS

1
introducing the computer

Ever since the second world war the computer has increasingly become used as an everyday tool, to the extent now that the majority of people have some connection with it in either their professional or private lives. While it is obvious that not everyone wishes to be associated with computer operation, there are numerous reasons for understanding its workings and the contribution it can make in various situations. A knowledge of the computer offers a certain degree of protection against its abuse and misapplication, while at the same time enabling one to recognise those situations where its use would be beneficial. It is equally important to know enough to justify its use as it is to explain its inappropriateness. We shall therefore begin by considering the computer and how it works, and then go on to discuss systems analysis and design. As stated previously, we intend our book as a simple introduction and not as a comprehensive textbook on the subject.

TYPES OF COMPUTER

There are two types of computer and although library applications demand the use of only one of those it will be as well to be acquainted with both types. The two types are a) analogue and b) digital.

THE ANALOGUE COMPUTER accepts information for processing in physical form, *ie* in terms of weight, volume, electric current, etc. It performs calculations on the incoming information according to a predetermined pattern which is usually represented by mechanical, electro-mechanical or electronic units. The results of the calculations usually appear in a similar form to the input. This computer is built to satisfy a particular requirement and can usually only be used for this one purpose. This makes it unsuitable for library requirements which necessitate that data be processed and recorded in quite a different way. These computers are used mostly for scientific work.

THE DIGITAL COMPUTER accepts information for processing in a unitary form, *ie* letters, symbols and numbers. These may represent anything the computer user wishes. All calculations or processing of the incoming data is carried out in digital form, thus all the usual mathematical rules and functions may be applied, and the results are printed out in conventional letters, symbols or numbers. The digital computer is therefore a general purpose computer, particularly suited to commercial applications and information processing in general, and it is this computer which will be discussed throughout our book.

The digital computer can be categorised under two headings according to the mode of operation: *1*) batch processor and *2*) real-time processor.

BATCH PROCESSOR

Designed to process data which has been accumulated into groups or batched over a period of time. We will now look at the components of such a computer under four main headings. These components or units, known as the *hardware* are the machinery which carries out the instructions necessary to perform the jobs to be done. FIGURE 1 illustrates the configuration of a batch processor. We will consider each unit according to the flow of work, that is the order in which incoming data would be processed.

The input units

The function of the input units is to convert the data presented to them into a form which is acceptable to the central processor. Data may be presented to a computer in a number of ways, each using a unique coding system for the representation of data. It is because the central processor will only accept data in a standard form that input conversion units are required. These units will be considered in detail in the next chapter.

The central processor

From the input units, data passes to a section of the store in the central processor and, once there, may be treated in any way desired. What happens at this stage, and at the input and output stages, is governed by the *program*. This is a series of instructions devised by the computer user or his agent, or by the computer manufacturer to perform certain tasks. The answer to the frequently asked question as to what can a computer do depends entirely on the instructions given in the programs which control its operation. There can be any number of programs written by programmers, but not all will be required for any one job. The appropriate ones are selected from a program library which, like any bibliographic collection, keeps all the programs recorded on reels of magnetic tape or sometimes on sets of punched cards, in the order most helpful to users (usually by program number) on open shelves or in cabinets. However, the difference between this library and a conventional one is that magnetic tape is sensitive to the dust and humidity content of the atmosphere, both of which have to be carefully controlled in the program library. Once the program has been selected it is fed into the program area of the store where it remains during the whole of the processing run.

Since a program has to contain all the instructions necessary to perform the job to which it relates, it follows that where a great number of instructions are required the list may be very long. The central processor has a stated capacity measured in approximately thousands (K) of units. These units may consist of one character, or of two numerical or one other type of character (called a *byte*), or of more than two characters (called a computer *word*). This means that the processor will handle data either by characters, bytes, or words which would be a number of characters taken together. Since program instructions are a series of characters, there are often too many for the capacity of that part of the store allotted to the program. Where this is the case the program can be fed in by segments.

Part of the central processor is the *control unit*. This picks up one program instruction at a time and activates the necessary circuits to enable the rest of the processor, the input and output units, and the storage units to perform the required tasks. Besides the control provided by the program, a more direct control over the operation of the computer is exercised by the computer operator panel or typewriter *console*. By this means the operator is able to key in messages to start a program run. The console also provides messages from the processor which tell the operator when runs have been completed, when faults occur, and keep him generally informed about what is going on inside the computer. Some programs may include instructions for messages to be passed to the operator during the run.

The last part of the central processor is the *arithmetic unit*. This carries out additions, subtractions or comparisons. Using just these three basic functions it is possible, with special programs, to carry out complex mathematical calculations.

Output units

Once an amount of processing designated by the program has occurred, the resultant data is passed to the output units. The output form varies according to the type of unit used. The most common record form is print, which is readily usable, though often a machine readable form is used, thus enabling it to act as input later. This latter may be punched out on cards or paper tape or stored on some magnetic recording medium. Print may be carried out by a line printer or using some photographic method which outputs from magnetic tapes onto microfilm or film for use as intermediate masters for conventional printing systems.

Backing store/units

The backing store can be regarded as the filing system for the computer. The store comprises a magnetic recording medium such as tape or disc, though there are other storage methods which will be discussed in the next chapter. Magnetic tape reels can be kept, so enabling cumulative files to be made available on as many reels as necessary. Small discs and disc packs are also exchangeable in that they can be removed from the disc unit and kept. These extra storage units are necessary since it is impossible for the central processor working store to be used for long term storage. This part, which is always cleared before each program is run, is the most expensive part of a computer and cannot be used economically for permanent storage. The use of the working store is therefore restricted to the temporary storage of data being received from the input units, the data awaiting output and to the performance of calculations.

The digital computer offers marked advantages in the speed of processing. Each program instruction is carried out in a fraction of a second. The input, output and backing store units, all of which are electro-mechanical *ie* involving some physical movement, are obviously slower than the electronic devices of the central processor. This latter may be looked upon as the heart of the computer, while the units are known as the *peripherals*. Computer operating speeds have increased considerably but the peripherals still require the lowest units of measurement. Speeds are expressed as follows:

Electro-mechanical = one thousandth of a second
= one millisecond = ms

Electronic = one millionth of a second
= microsecond = μs

or = one thousand-millionth of a second
= nanosecond = ns

To give an example of the speed of the central processor, the time required to carry out the program instructions necessary to add two four-digit numbers would be approximately 10μs, and it would therefore take one second to carry out 100,000 such calculations.

REAL-TIME PROCESSOR

The main difference between a batch and real-time processor is in the input and output units used. Real-time processors intended to handle the large volumes of data associated with the batch method. The units are connected to the computer enabling direct entry of data into the processor. Such connection is termed *on-line,* and the units so connected are called *terminals*. The terminal is often an electric typewriter on which an operator can key in information or a question, within a given format, without the need to present such information on machine readable media such as punched cards. A program will control the processing of data received from a terminal, adding it to the files on backing store or referring to the data already on file for transmission back to the terminal. As with the batch processor all calculations take place in the working store. This type of processor, one of which is illustrated in FIGURE 2, provides a quick response to interrogations which may be received from a number of terminals.

Many digital computers are designed to run more than one program at a time. These *multi-program machines* are usually large, having large capacity central processors, and are consequently very expensive. The need for a large capacity processor is dictated by the fact that there will be many programs which have to be held in the program store at the same time. A large processor also offers advantages in that the various parts of the computer will be used to the maximum efficiency since the differences in their operating speeds can be offset by switching from one program to another and back again in a fraction of a second and thus fill any waiting time. Such processing is controlled by a special program supplied by the makers of the machine, and known as the *operating system.*

Since computers are complex and high speed machines there is also the need to provide some means of knowing when they are not operating correctly. Every computer has a checking system built in to the circuitry and should any malfunction or failure occur the program run will stop automatically. This situation often seems very much in doubt when jobs given to the computer fail to be completed as expected. Although computers sometimes fail to recognise a fault in operation, most mistakes in processing or output are due to human error when writing the programs or designing the system.

As a last point in our overall look at a computer configuration there are two common terms with which the reader should be fully acquainted. The first is the term *hardware,* which was mentioned on page 12. This refers to all the machinery involved, specifically the computer itself and all the peripheral equipment and terminals. The second term is *software* which refers to the programs and all the documentation connected with the computer systems.

2
data carriers and the peripherals

Since we have not yet arrived at the happy situation where the computer could accept data by our speaking directly to it or scribbling on a piece of paper, it is necessary to understand the way in which information can be fed into, and received back from the computer. We shall therefore look at the media which carry the data and the machines which handle them. Not every computer requires the data to be coded onto a special input medium before being fed in. Some permit data to be keyed in direct to the computer. However, the former method is the more usual, particularly in cases where a large amount of data is concerned, since preparation can be done away from the computer installation and can be batched. Batches are fed into the computer when they have reached a size sufficiently large to warrant a processing run. The three most common media are: Punched cards, Punched paper tape, Magnetic tape.

PUNCHED CARDS

Since punched cards have been a popular data carrier for some 80 years, there is a considerable range of equipment available besides the computer to process them. The card is divided into 80 columns, each of which may be used to record one character whether a letter, number or symbol. Most characters have a standard punching code and an example is shown in FIGURE 3. It will be seen that one or more holes in a column will be punched out to represent the desired character, and that there are in all twelve such punching positions in each column.

A number of columns can be grouped together for recording a multi-digit number or a word. Where such numbers or words relate collectively to one part of the data, as might be the case with an accessions number or the title statement, such a grouping is referred to as a field. The layout of data on cards will be dealt with in the chapter on input procedures. The data for processing therefore is punched into cards, checked, and then when there are sufficient cards in the batch, fed into the computer.

PUNCHED PAPER TAPE

Unlike cards which are now a standard size, paper tape can vary in width. On tape, characters are represented by holes punched across its width. Each width or 'frame', equivalent to a punched card column, consists of a number of punching positions or *tracks*. A code used to represent some characters is shown in FIGURE 4. The usual recording density for paper tape is 10 characters to the inch. Since paper tape is used with a variety of equipment like accounting machines, tape-typewriters, Telex, as well as computer systems, the widths and character codes have not been fully standardised. However, two widths are being adopted more or less as standard, namely five and eight track tape. With eight track tape only seven are used to hold the character code while the eighth is reserved for machine checking purposes and is known as the *parity* track. According to whether the parity is to be even or odd, the number of holes in each frame will also be either always even or always odd. To achieve this the punching machine will automatically add a hole in the parity track if the character code does not fulfil this requirement.

MAGNETIC TAPE

Although there are various widths, magnetic tape is usually half an inch wide, consisting of a plastic base, the coating of which can be magnetised. A character is represented by magnetic spots across the width of the tape similar to the holes on paper tape, as illustrated in FIGURE 5. However, being magnetic, the tape can accommodate varying numbers of characters to the inch according to the equipment used for recording, and an example of layout for variable length data is shown in FIGURE 6. The packing density, as it is called, is usually 200, 556 or 800 characters per inch, though even higher densities are now being introduced. As with tape on a recorder, data can be erased so that the tape can be used many times. However, due to the high speeds at which it operates, the recording surface does eventually become unreliable after constant use.

THE PERIPHERALS: INPUT UNITS

Card reader

Once data or program instructions have been punched into 80 column cards which are usually in the correct order, they are then placed in the card reader. Each card in turn is read either column by column or row by row, *ie* from top of bottom. The cards pass under the reading head which sense the holes photo-electrically and cause appropriate signals to be sent to the central processor store. Cards can be read at a constant rate or in short bursts. The speeds at which readers operate vary considerably, and the computer purchaser will choose whichever is considered most suitable for the intended operating conditions. His choice can range between readers of 400 and 1,000 cards a minute. Although cards are quite tough they are subject to wear, and therefore if passed through the reader too often may eventually foul up the reading process. For speed it is customary to transfer the data on cards to magnetic tape as soon as possible.

Paper tape reader

One feature of paper tape is that the data punched on will always remain in the original order, so there is never any need to devise ways of checking that the sequence is correct. The reader senses the holes in each frame, usually by means of photo-electric cells. Most readers can accept tapes using 5, 6, 7 or 8 tracks. Since the tape is in one long stream, the program controls the amount read at one time, passing the data on to the central processor store. Again speeds vary, but range between 400 and 1,000 character positions a second. Note that any blanks between punch frames have to be reckoned in when calculating the speed.

Magnetic tape decks

Reels of tape containing data have to be loaded onto high speed readers known as *decks*. These are capable of passing the tape across the reading head at rates in excess of 100 inches per second. However, this does not tell one the reading speed, since the way the data is spread along the tape and the packing density used will determine this. Details of the deck will be found in the next chapter.

THE PERIPHERALS: OUTPUT UNITS

When the program has completed certain stages of its work, it will obey output instructions indicating what is to be done with the resultant data. These will be brought out of the working store and fed to one of the output units, a backing store or both.

Card punch

Selected data may be output onto punched cards. This operation would require certain program instructions which would have to transfer the data into one or more unpunched cards. This is a relatively slow method of output since computer card punches operate at speeds usually ranging from 100 to 300 cards a minute, and to use this method for large amounts of data would slow down the general operating speed of the computer. Because of this most computer systems include a means of 'buffering' data awaiting to be output. This enables the central processor to operate at its usual speed and the resultant data is put in an assigned buffer area in one of the stores temporarily until the output unit can receive them. Output on cards would of course only be required when the data has to be machine read at some later stage.

Paper tape punch

This is also a slow method of output, working at between 20 and 120 characters a second. The only reason for requiring output in this form is that the resultant data is required elsewhere in machine readable form. Paper tape, being cheap, compact and relatively light, is very suitable for posting any distance, while cards are much heavier and always run the risk of being dropped or damaged which could render them useless for input.

Line printer

Certainly the most common output form is the printed version using high speed line printers. These can accept a range of paper sizes, plain, ruled or pre-printed, with or without copies. The overall width of the paper can vary between 4 and 20 inches. It is possible to produce up to six copies from one printing using inter-leaved carbon paper, carbon backed papers or those incorporating micro-encapsulated dyes. Paper is supplied already made up into the set required and is in one continuous folded strip. The folds allow a sheet or page to be a maximum of 20 inches deep. Even the widest paper will not provide more than a 16 inch line of print giving 10 characters to the inch. The more usual depth of lined page is 10 inches which allows 60 lines of print.

There are two basic types of mechanical line printer, the most common is the *barrel* or *drum* printer, and the other is the *chain* printer. The most significant difference between the two is the range of characters which they offer. With the former the characters form part of the surface of the barrel and it is therefore necessary to change the entire barrel to obtain a different character set. The barrel usually offers between 48 and 64 characters including the alphabet (upper case only), the numbers 0-9 and a variety of symbols. The characters are ranged round the barrel, one set for each printing position. Thus there will be 160 sets to match the 160 print positions along the paper. There are also 160 hammers ranged along the print line behind the paper. Printing speed is usually 1,000 lines a minute, but speeds of up to 1,500 a minute are available. The high speed is achieved by printing on the fly. This is the continuous rotation of the barrel while the hammers located behind the paper strike it onto the character at the precise moment when the hammer, print line and character are aligned. However, because the barrel rotates at such high speed the character may not be accurately positioned on the line. This is the reason for some computer printout having lines akin to the proverbial dog's leg.

With a chain printer it is possible to have up to 240 character positions by having complete groups of characters repeated in the chain. One type of print chain can accommodate up to 192 different characters. The chain revolves horizontally across the paper and there is therefore a waiting time while the appropriate part of the chain reaches each print position. Obviously the delay is less if the character group is repeated round the chain. As with the barrel printer, the paper passes between the characters and a bank of hammers. Operating speeds range between 150 and 1,000 lines a minute. The character set can be made specially, but is usually particularly well suited to carry upper and lower case. Where necessary more than one chain can be provided though the printer is only able to take one at a time. By this method the printing of more than one type of alphabet is possible.

3
the peripherals continued

BACKING STORE UNITS

The backing store units of most computers are either magnetic tape decks or disc drives. Unless the files of data are kept permanently on a fixed disc or a drum, it will be necessary for the operator to select the required files from the file library, and load these onto the appropriate unit. The program can then extract data from the files when necessary and read this into the working store. When we say data is 'read' from disc or tape we mean that it is copied into the store so that the original remains unaltered. Because systems using computers have to recognise the dictates of magnetic tapes and discs we shall now go on to look at these two media in some detail.

MAGNETIC TAPE DECKS

The data on magnetic tape is grouped into fields, records and blocks, as shown previously in FIGURE 6. Characters are grouped together to form a *field* in the same way as with cards or paper tape. This group may represent a number or words. In most cases it is necessary to use a number of these fields to form what is called a *record.* An example of a record might be an accession number followed by author, title and imprint. In turn these records are grouped together to form *blocks.* There are two good reasons why records, if they are short and do not contain many characters, should be treated in blocks. Firstly, the working store may well be capable of accepting more information than is contained in one record, thereby wasting time if only one is read at a time. Secondly, the way in which the tape deck operates could make the reading of single records a slow and uneconomical process. Like the fields and records which form them, the blocks can vary in length. Data is not put on the tape in a continuous stream, but is arranged in blocks of stated maximum length which are separated by unmagnetised sections of tape. These sections, referred to as *inter-block gaps,* are necessary because the speed at which the tape moves is critical. When the program reaches an instruction requiring data to be written on the tape, the deck has to be allowed time to start the normally stationary tape moving, accelerating it to the correct speed. Only at this speed can data be read from or written to the tape During the acceleration time prior to writing, some unmagnetised tape will have passed the writing head and it is this portion which forms one part of the inter-block gap. The rest of the gap occurs during deceleration after all the data in the block has been written out.

The significance of the gap must be considered when deciding how many records shall form a block. With very short blocks the tape deck will spend a disproportionate amount of time stopping and starting, while a wasteful amount of the tape will not be carrying data. For example, if blocks were only 80 characters long, which is the total capacity of a punched card, only 20 percent of the tape would carry data, while the rest would be wasted on inter-block gaps. Such a block size would also slow down the reading speed to 15 percent of the possible speed. It is thus usual to make blocks as large as possible commensurate with the capacity of the store which would have to receive them when being read. The tape will then read into store one block for each read instruction occurring in the program.

When the reel is mounted on the deck, the tape runs from the feed reel, and then passes an erase head, a write head and a read head, as illustrated in FIGURE 7. The first is used when the tape is to be cleared before writing new data on to it. The other two are used to record data and to detect it respectively. These two are often referred to as the *read/write head* because the magnets which do these jobs are in one housing. The vacuum reservoirs are to ensure that there are always two loops in the tape, to take up any surge during starting and stopping. When the program has finished with the tape, it is rewound onto the original spool at up to three times the speed of reading or writing. Reels usually contain 1,200, 2,400 or 3,600 foot lengths of tape. When moving at the correct speed of over 100 inches per second, data can be transferred between deck and store at the rate of between 20-160 thousand characters per second. The total number of characters likely to be on a 2,400 foot reel, allowing for inter-block gaps, would be approximately 12 million.

One disadvantage of magnetic tape is the serial arrangement of the data. This means that blocks required situated at the end of the tape can only be reached after the program has read in every previous block on the tape and rejected them. For this reason due consideration has to be given to the way in which data is organised in the files.

Once the reel has been loaded and the tape deck switched on, the program will begin by reading the first block. This is always an identifier which ensures that the correct reel is being used. This prevents wanted data being accidentally overwritten or the wrong data being processed. Once the check has proved satisfactory the processing begins block by block.

EXCHANGEABLE DISCS

The data on a disc store is written on a series of concentric bands on the surface of each disc. The bands are divided into a number of blocks or sections as illustrated in FIGURE 8. It is possible to process each block on the disc separately, which gives this form of storage a distinct advantage over tape. It may be quicker to reach any block while the sequence in which they are called up or accessed is not critical. These two points have to be borne in mind when choosing a storage system.

Each disc has two surfaces, just like the long-playing record, and a pack or cartridge of six are stacked permanently on a vertical spindle (see FIGURE 9). There are also single disc units available.

When the disc pack is loaded into the unit and the lid closed, the discs revolve continuously together at some 2,400 revolutions per minute. Discs vary in size but are usually about 14 inches in diameter. In each pack two of the disc surfaces are reserved for the disc system control, leaving ten surfaces on which to record data. This gives a typical pack the capacity of some 4 million characters with 100 bands or 8 million with 200 bands. Exchangeable disc packs are now available with considerably higher capacities. The data can be transferred, once the correct block has been located, at some 66 thousand characters a second.

OTHER FORMS OF STORE

Other less common forms of backing store are:

Drums: permanently mounted vertically or horizontally, having data recorded on, or read from, the surface while the drum continuously revolves at high speed.

Fixed discs: operating in the same way as disc packs but permanently mounted vertically or horizontally and having a very much greater capacity, some are over 400 million characters.

Magnetic cards: having recording strips down the length of the oblong card sometimes using edge notched coding to permit automatic selection from a cartridge.

The various units in these two chapters have been regarded as optional, since the purchaser of a computer may select from a wide range, those peripherals most suited to the system required. In some cases peripherals may be duplicated, for example there might be a case for two line printers. Any limitation on the number of peripherals connected to the computer depends largely on the number of special channels fitted into the central processor.

OTHER METHODS OF INPUT AND OUTPUT

The methods described so far of feeding data into a computer and for obtaining output are those most frequently encountered in computer systems. This is not an exclusive list, and therefore a number of other forms are mentioned here since they could be of interest to those concerned with computer systems for library applications.

CHARACTER RECOGNITION

Specialised readers can be used to input data whereby only documents printed in a specific typeface can be passed through the reader. An example of one such typeface used for character recognition is that used for the numbers printed along the bottom of bank cheques. These characters can be read by a magnetic ink character reader. Non-magnetic character typefaces can be recognised by optical character readers, and these latter have more flexibility.

TERMINALS

These can act as both input and output units to any real-time system. They include a simple electric typewriter, or even a tape deck, which can carry out both functions, or such units as a card reader, paper tape reader, or line printer, which are able to carry out only one function. The terminals can be situated many miles from the computer, connections being effected via telephone cables. The data passes from the terminal into a modulator/demodulator unit, usually abbreviated to *modem,* which converts the signal into the form required for transmission. When the signal is received it is converted back by another modem as illustrated in FIGURE 10. Most systems can transmit to or from a terminal using the same cable. When the cable is not being used for this purpose, it can revert to its normal role as a telephone line.

The use of terminals is increasing each year as they enable the calculating and storage capacity of a large computer to be made available at a large number of places on request. Thus it is possible to set up central data banks which would be available for interrogation at many points at the same time. The terminals for such a system would probably be the typewriter or a visual display unit, a small television tube, where the question is keyed in on a keyboard and the answer is displayed on the tube as writing or a line diagram.

4
software

The function of the program has been mentioned earlier, and it is important to appreciate that the efficient use of the hardware depends on programs of different types. These programs, together with all documentation associated with computer systems, are known as *software,* and can be classed under the following headings: user programs, programming aids, supervisory or executive programs and operating systems, and applications packages. User programs would be written by programmers on the library staff or in specialist agencies, in order to produce the particular output needed by that library. The other three types are termed standard programs as they can be used by anyone who has access to the type of computer for which they have been specifically written. Since they are related more to a make of computer than a particular job, the manufacturers generally prepare these programs and make them available to their customers, sometimes without charge. Such programs may also be developed by specialist organisations such as universities, government establishments or industry, and at a later stage made available for purchase. The value of such programs is that they satisfy many of the basic requirements of computer users, thus avoiding duplication of programming effort. Whenever considering the use of a computer, it is therefore wise to find out what software is already available from the manufacturer or elsewhere, to determine what may be used or adapted to meet expected requirements. Let us now look at the four types of program.

USER PROGRAMS

These programs are prepared by the computer user to suit the special requirements of his system. Many such programs may be prepared to perform different jobs. When they have been tested, and proved satisfactory, they are stored on magnetic tape or disc as part of the program library. Since these programs are the responsibility of the user it is useful to know what is involved in their preparation.

The purpose of any program is to process data which is made available via input units or from backing stores. Before writing, the programmer will require details of media or file layout, with regard to field headings, field sizes, special tags and so on for all input data, as well as for stored data. Also required will be the exact format and type of output. These details would result from systems design and be given as the *program specification*. The importance of these details should be stressed since failure to define them comprehensively can entail many wasted hours of programming effort. Once provided with this information, the programmer begins by working out the logical steps of the program. To assist him he will set out these steps in a flowchart, using the symbols as given in FIGURE 11, showing the sequence of instructions. An example of a flowchart is shown in FIGURE 12.

The computer works by progressing at high speed through a series of simple steps logically arranged. It is the programmer who decides on the steps necessary and their sequence. Failure of the program to achieve intended results most often arises from the omission of steps or from a fault in the logic of the sequence. In a short linear sequence such errors may be easy to detect. However, with programs requiring the processing to flow, according to certain conditions, through one of a number of sequences (called *subroutines*) or to repeat certain sequences (called *loops*), the detection of errors becomes a matter of considerable skill.

The next stage is conversion of the flowchart steps into instructions or statements which can be fed into the computer as the program. This is the coding process. These instructions are written using a system of coding, acceptable to the machine, known as a *programming language*. This may be *low level*, being in the exact form required by the control units of the computer. The language is said to be machine based when it can only be used with the computer for which it has been specifically designed. Such would be PLAN (programming language nineteen hundred) used only with the ICL

1900 series machines. It usually takes longer to prepare a program using a low level language since each program instruction will nearly equal a machine instruction, but generally the resultant program is more efficient. A *high level* language is problem oriented, in that it is devised for ease of writing rather than for any specific computer. It is easier to use and speeds up program writing since many machine instructions may be represented by just one program instruction. It is, though, sometimes less efficient than the low level language. Typical high level languages which can be used with most modern computers are:

COBOL (COmmon Business Oriented Language)—widely used for processing commercial data and incorporating many natural language terms.

FORTRAN (FORmula TRANslator) and ALGOL (ALGOrithmic Language)—Both used for scientific and some commercial data. Instructions are written in mathematical symbols. There is another high level language called PL/1, which combines the advantages of COBOL and FORTRAN. At the time of writing this cannot be used with all computers.

After coding the program onto punching sheets, it is given to an operator for encoding onto some input medium such as punched cards. The program is then fed into the computer for testing. Where high level languages have been used, the program instructions have to be translated into machine format. This operation is known as *compilation* and is carried out by a special compiler program. High level language programs have to be compiled before they can be tested. The testing is done by making the program process test data, and then checking the results. It is rarely possible to write an error free program at the first attempt. Only when the program has been fully tested and all errors corrected does the programmer's responsibility for it cease.

Programming aids

Because compilers enable programmers to make use of high level languages, they are one of the most useful programming aids available. The compilers are written by the computer manufacturer and supplied as the link between the unique format requirements of their hardware and the high level language of internationally agreed formats and standards. Although a program written in COBOL should ideally run on any computer for which there is a COBOL compiler, this is rarely the case in practice, which is because each manufacturer writes the compiler for only a selection of all the possible COBOL statements. It is therefore necessary for the programmer to be familiar with any particular requirements of the computer before starting to write the program.

The compilation process requires that the user program be fed into the computer on cards or similar medium. Cards are used most often since any corrections can be achieved by mere replacement of cards. The compiler will take each COBOL instruction and write onto magnetic tape an equivalent set of instructions in machine code. The compiler also checks for mistakes such as invalid terms or symbols, and certain omissions. All the COBOL instructions are listed by the printer, together with error messages, as the compilation progresses. As at input each instruction is punched onto a separate card, so the listing will display them one on each line. A small program, which says nothing of length of time it would take to run, could run to some few hundred instructions, while a large one may involve thousands. To correct errors, on-line terminals may be used or new cards made, so that incorrect cards are replaced with correct ones. The program is then compiled again. This process continues until the program is error free. Unfortunately correct compilation only means that the program is acceptable to the computer. It does not indicate that the program will perform the required function. It is thus necessary to run the program against test data to check that it performs correctly and does not contain errors of logic.

The other type of software is the sub-routine, one of which is the diagnostic routine assisting the programmer to discover errors. A sub-routine is a series of program instructions written so that they may be incorporated in any program when required. These are written for either mathematical calculations or sorting data into a sequence. An extensive list of sub-routines is available with most computers.

SUPERVISORY OR EXECUTIVE PROGRAMS AND OPERATING SYSTEMS

The supervisory or executive program is held in the program store whenever the computer is in use. Its function is to load the user program from the input or backing store into the program store. While the user program is running, the executive program is responsible for the operation of all input, output and storage devices. Should there be a failure in any part of the machine system, the run is stopped automatically by the executive program and a message displayed on the operator console. The executive also maintains a complete log of each program run by displaying on the console the name of that program, peripheral units used, errors occurring and the length of the run. Such information is needed by the computer manager who has to account for its use. The length of time taken also needs to be known when jobs are charged out to different users. This is most likely to apply if the library is using a computer not directly under its own control.

If a computer can handle many user programs at once, known as a *multiprogram machine,* the amount of housekeeping or self-maintenance needed is considerably increased. This is achieved by another program called the *operating system* which is complementary to the executive program. This will control the scheduling of program runs so that there is always a user program with its data ready to be loaded for processing. As soon as one run is completed the operating system will load the next program in the queue, ensuring that the necessary peripherals are free. If they are not available another program will be selected for which peripherals are available immediately. An important job can be given a high priority so that the run will be made as soon as possible at the expense of other programs which may be running at the same time. A further function of the operating system is to control the use of terminals with real-time processing. It makes a constant check of all terminals to detect when one becomes live, thus ensuring that there is a user program in the store to respond to the incoming message and arranging any file interrogation which may be necessary.

The operating system is a large, complex program which would therefore take up a lot of store space. To prevent this, it is usually written in modular form, the modules being called in from a backing store by a master program held permanently in store. The operating system allows the computer to be used efficiently by making certain that there is the minimum of delay between each job.

APPLICATION PACKAGES

Complete programs or suites of programs can be written to carry out a task which may be common to a number of users. These are called application packages and can be regarded as complete programs in themselves. For these, data have to be laid out in a stated format. There are few packages for library application as yet. However, with the continuing effort to establish MARC (Machine Readable Catalogue) as an internationally acceptable format for the exchange of bibliographic records, packages should become available for library housekeeping routines.

PROGRAMS AND THE STORE

When discussing the merits of various programming languages, the reader will detect a concern for the amount of store space required for programs. This chapter will have demonstrated that the executive programs, operating system and the user programs may be competing for store space. It is this conflict which can influence a decision on the language to be used. The high level language, as has been explained, hides many machine instructions in each statement so that what appears to be a relatively short program may really need an inordinate amount of store space once compiled.

5
concerning systems analysis

Since we have explained the way in which a computer performs the tasks we give to it, there may be a temptation to look upon this machine as the obvious answer to virtually every work situation. Certainly when time on the computer is offered, and general opportunities for computer use are presented, there would seem to be every reason to seek out jobs which could be turned over to the machine. At the time such adventurousness may seem to have merit, if only to show that the library is keeping up with the twentieth century or to relieve immediate work loads. As the use of the computer is inevitably extended, the limitation of such a piecemeal policy may become apparent and lead to the realisation that the way in which the library operates has to be viewed as an overall concept if work is to flow smoothly and services are to run at their most effective. It is for this reason that the design or re-design of the whole library system is a matter for the systems analyst. It should be realised immediately that an investigation does not at all presage the use of a machine of any kind. It is therefore not the case that systems analysis is concerned solely with the use or introduction of computers. The purpose of analysis is to optimise design in whatever way this may be achieved. But having said this, it must also be admitted that the systems analyst is associated more with those situations likely to require a computer than with any others. This arises because the efficient use of the computer rests on the satisfactory exploitation of its potential.

What is meant by the words system and analysis? A system may be defined as a network of operations involving people, equipment and documents, which processes given inputs to produce required outputs. The difficulty which arises here is the identification of the limits of any network in order to define our system. The levels at which a network of operations occur can almost be chosen at random. Choosing the public library as an example, one might select the acquisitions department network and treat this as a system. However, this department is merely a part of the total library service of the area, which in turn may be regarded as a part of the public library service or local government services. Whatever we choose to call the system, there will always be some parts of the network which connect with other systems. This is why it is quite valid and possible to select the loans operations and discuss this network as a system despite the fact that it is obviously only one facet of the total library system. Thus to arrive at a workable level, it is necessary to determine the operations which are to be considered together and which would be designated the 'system', and then to identify groups of operations which form networks within the total system. Such group may be designated 'sub-systems'.

Analysis might be defined as the examination of an existing system or the requirements of one not yet in existence, in order to evaluate the methods, resources, products and costs of such a system. To achieve such an evaluation, the analyst will have to look at every part of the system to understand the way in which each relates to the other, and to determine the contribution which each makes to the system. In each case the following may be considered: —

Operations
Personnel
Materials
Equipment
Documentation
Work flow
Relationships
Costs

Operations: Any activity which takes place at any level is an operation. However, it is useful to classify operations to assist in adjudging the qualifications or skills required to execute them. Gilchrist (1968) presents a helpful guide to the way in which library operations might be graded. Thus 'processing' may be regarded as a sub-system, while cataloguing would be classed as a 'procedure' under it, but duplicating the catalogue cards would be classed as a task.

Personnel: Not only is it necessary to note the number and type of staff required to carry out operations, but also to discover the formal and the informal structure through which communication channels operate. There is a tendency to assume that the declared structure is also the effective one. Closer examination of communication habits may elicit a quite different network. The so called grapevine has often proved a faster and an equally accurate communication system as the formal channels.

Materials: Naturally the commodities handled will affect the design of the system. Monographs have well established routines for handling, but newer formats are still insufficiently tried out. Thus some microforms and magnetically recorded data carriers may require systems radically different from those coping with monographs. Also in cases where the recorded information includes some which is security classified the system would naturally reflect the required restrictions.

Equipment: Whatever is used to aid human effort may be considered under this head, whether paper clips or computers. The ubiquitous rubber stamp which is an essential tool for so many jobs will have to be duly noted both as to when it is used and what information it impresses.

Documentation: Attached to every part of the system will be certain documents either containing instructions or conveying information generated as a consequence of some operation. Under this head would be included all the forms or printed stationery which are used to record information, details of their number, frequency, authorisation and distribution.

Work flow: The way in which the work is sequenced and the rate at which it progresses in each part of the system tells much about its efficiency. Work badly routed or flowing at unpredictable and uneven rates can do much to undermine conscientious human effort.

Relationships: Even a minor task is performed as a contribution to the general effort of achieving the goals of the system. It is thus necessary to determine the relationship between the various levels within the system and between the various activities. This enables one to decide which relationships are dependent, which interdependent and which contributory.

Costs: Not only would one be concerned with the costs of the materials, equipment, personnel, etc but also those connected with an activity, the time it takes and the relative value which it might be said to have as a contribution to system performance.

Many of the points of investigation would seem to be more familiarly associated with organisation and methods studies and the like. It is not surprising that the analysis of a system should make use of many well tried techniques such as work measurement, time and motion study and so on. What needs to be recognised is the fact that these techniques produce data which form only a part of the whole analysis results. It should also be realised that the systems analyst will be expected to use such results to design a new system overall.

Having explained what the systems analyst does we are faced with the question of who best should serve in this capacity in the library situation. It must be clear that the person undertaking the job will need to be well versed in the methods of analysis. This is an obvious prerequisite for any appointment. Whether the analyst needs to have any knowledge of the way in which libraries operate could be a matter of debate, but it should be stressed that a good analyst is used to apprising himself fully of the workings of completely new situations. The danger of using someone versed in library practices is that such a person would find it very difficult to approach the analysis and design with a completely open mind. Inevitably prejudged issues and traditional standpoints would be very hard to avoid, while the outsider would be more likely to view each part of an existing system without any preconceptions associated with the long standing debates over methodology or value. It is the outside and unbiased view which is the essential part of a good analysis. Throughout the investigation the analyst will want to know why a given operation is performed at all, and then why it is performed in a given way. Such questioning can all too easily become a formality when the analyst is someone for whom certain operations have become an accepted part of a library system. Perhaps an equally important consideration is the freedom which the analyst must be given to investigate wherever and however he sees fit. This means that to appoint someone already within the organisation or someone from outside who is to become a member of the staff may in turn mean that the required freedom is never realised. A consultant who is completely unconnected with the organisation and who will not be joining it has nothing to lose by any proposition or demand he may decide to make. He would be free to talk at most levels without the constraints which rank would inevitably introduce. An impartial and thoroughly objective assessment of the system is the one most likely to give rise to a satisfactory design. Less readily admitted by those who have to take action on the final report, is the attitude which is elicited according to the identity of the author of that report. When made by someone known in the library world to hold certain views about given operations or structures, then the recommendations may well be regarded with some scepticism. At the same time the analyst who has no previous experience of a library system may find his recommendations being viewed with some scepticism on the grounds that he cannot be expected to understand fully the historic reasons for the way in which parts of the existing system operate. The way to overcome this dilemma might be the appointment of an outside analyst to whom would be attached an experienced member of the staff who would be directly connected with the implementation and operation of the new system. This goes some way to removing the possible objections which might be raised to any radical changes proposed. More important is the value which is derived from having someone on the staff who has an intimate knowledge of the system design. Nevertheless questions will always arise over modifications or developments as the system changes.

6

preparatory steps to analysis

The whole approach to analysis has to be carefully planned, and executed with some regard to time, cost, manpower and the possible disruption to current work flow. To begin with there is good reason for taking a rather cautious approach. Not everyone in the organisation, even at the higher management levels, may agree with the need or see the desirability of a new system. This feeling may be aggravated if it is intended that the new system will make considerable use of the computer, particularly so if this move results in redundancies. Computer use has not been without its difficulties, and certainly in libraries there has been rather less than enthusiasm for its installation. It is thus a wise policy for the analyst to detect at an early stage the quarters from which opposition or unhelpfulness might be expected during the course of investigations. One might therefore give four headings as the first steps in analysis:

1 Determine the objectives of the new system.
2. Draw up a preliminary report.
3 Obtain management agreement.
4 Publicise the analysis programme.

I DETERMINING THE OBJECTIVES

A tale is told of an organisation which convened a meeting to discuss in detail the objectives of the library system, so that the analyst could determine the overall purpose of the system he was expected to design. Some weeks later the meeting was adjourned, it having been decided that to outline the objectives of a library system without knowing the design was impossible. It will be appreciated that the commercial enterprise or the government department has an inherent purpose around which the system will be designed. In the case of a library service there is no ideal except the generalisation that the user be provided with everything he needs. However, it is well known that many users are unsure of their needs, and we are therefore faced with discovering whether the user's declared requirement is the same as his actual requirement. Even when this matter has been clarified, we are no nearer a decision concerning the best way in which the need may be satisfied. Even worse, the value of such satisfaction and consequently the amount which might legitimately be spent in this connection is still in debate. Small wonder then that a discussion to determine the objectives of the library service can prove indecisive.

It is obvious that any organisation deciding to run a library service has already accepted the need for one. It then remains to decide what the extent of that service is to be. This need not depend at all on the declared needs of users but on the needs discovered as a result of the analysis. Nor yet need the service be limited by economic considerations until the cost of a recommended service has been assessed. However, this is not very helpful in a public library situation where users are too various and their needs too differing to provide any detailed guides for design. Such considerations as the siting of a library, the amount and the type of literature which may be demanded in a given area, can all be assessed, but many of the ancillary services may well be provided as a matter of policy, and not as a consequence of any discovered demand. Even in special library situations, where the organisation has taken a deliberate decision to establish a library, it is frequently found necessary to 'sell' the service to potential users. This suggests that such people, being unaware of their needs, would be unlikely to provide any useful criteria upon which to base specification recommendations. Those not familiar with the ways in which a library can serve them are often unable to visualise situations requiring one. The need to promote the library and to school potential users in the ways in which they can benefit from it may mean that such a service has to be designed to fulfill declared intentions rather than to meet inherent requirements.

Thus in a library situation one might start out with the declared intention of providing a complete library service at the personal level. In the light of the analysis findings this may prove unnecessary and too expensive when compared with the costs of other departments within the organisation. Equally as important as the objectives are the constraints. If the new system must operate in the existing buildings, or within a given budget or requiring no more than a given time on the computer, then obviously these limitations need to be known well before the design stage is reached.

2 THE PRELIMINARY REPORT

Having made some projections concerning the library service, it is possible to make rough estimates of the time, costs and manpower requirements of the analysis, design and implementation of the system. Naturally any organisation will view this more favourably when the estimates are presented promptly than in cases where the time and expense of the exercise exceed expectation. During the discussions with the management the analyst may discover that there is no conception of what a computer based system costs or involves. From the general outline elicited from the discussions on objectives, it should also be possible to make some very rough estimates to give management some indication of the scale of costs. For example, if objectives include using terminals on-line, it is possible to give estimates of their costs bearing in mind the extent to which they will be used.

The preliminary report also has to inform management of the ways in which the analysis will be carried out, so that full cooperation may be elicited from the organisation. Objections likely to come from those less convinced of the cause may also be ironed out at this stage before they gain strength or support.

3 MANAGEMENT AGREEMENT

Having fulfilled the above tasks one still needs management approval to be given publicly. This means that it accepts the terms of the exercise and is prepared to afford the analyst all the backing he may require in the event of non-cooperation at any point in the organisation. It is vitally important that the investigations which the analyst will be pursuing are known to have full management approval and for preference that approval should also be evident at the middle management level. Naturally in large organisations such decisions have to be formally channelled to those affected well before any action occurs. Too often the central sectors of a large complex have effective communication networks while the peripheral sectors find themselves ill informed and outside the general network. This situation can prove very unhelpful not only in relation to the acceptance of the analyst by the staff at these points, but also in relation to the cooperation which will be required.

4 PUBLICISING THE PROGRAMME

Since it will be necessary for the analyst and his team to visit many parts and people in the organisation, it is recommended that everyone should be made aware of the purpose of such an apparent intrusion. Until a detailed plan has been worked out, it will not be possible to decide which members of staff will be seen or for how long. It is therefore essential to warn everyone—even the most junior staff—that the analysis team may come to them for information about the jobs they do.

FIRST STEPS

Before the preliminary steps of the analysis, the analyst will want to recruit one or two people with whom he can share the supervision of data collection and analysis. As suggested earlier, such personnel are best taken from amongst the senior staff. Once recruited, the team then progresses to the first series of tasks. These are as follows:

Organisational structure: where none exists already, it will be necessary to make a structural chart showing the way in which the various departments or sections are interrelated and also the people responsible for those sections. Such a chart would appear similar to the one shown in FIGURE 13. This enables the existing structure to be categorised for the purposes of analysis and also identifies the the heads of the various sections who will be the first points of contact. It will assist generally in finding out the activities which occur in the departments and help to assess the communications network.

Documentation collection: organisations with an active personnel department (not usually the case with library systems) may be able to provide a considerable amount of documentation. Such things may be available as staff manuals, conditions of service, job descriptions, publicity material issued to staff, all of which help to inform the team about organisational structure and attitudes. Of particular value are the job descriptions which provide useful background material before interviewing and help to avoid wasting time with unnecessary questions. The informed interviewer usually gets better results. In the staff manuals explanations for practices which may not be understood will be found, and for responsibilities which have to be assigned in certain cases. Thus certain levels of activity may have to be handed over to more senior staff. Time wastage and misunderstanding can be avoided if such documentation is studied with some care.

Working plan: It is necessary to decide which areas are to be investigated first and how this investigation shall be carried out. Certainly the most fruitful approach if at all possible is a meeting of department heads so that all can be fully informed about the enquiry. At the same time it gives an early opportunity for them to meet the analyst and his team and to put questions. Once the plan of approach has been agreed, it is appropriate at this point to draw up a tentative time chart showing expected duration of enquiries and the order in which they may be undertaken. The chart may well be modified as the analysis progresses, but it does act as a provisional guide line.

Management check: Before launching out with the program the preparatory moves outlined above may have thrown up some points not raised at the first meeting with the management; *eg* whether security classified reports are to be included in any new system devised, or whether all the services now provided externally by the system are to continue in their present form.

Before leaving this chapter it should be stated that the term 'the management' has been used deliberately. It is recognised that in many library situations the librarian is not wholly responsible for the decisions about the service which he provides. It may well be that in the first instance the analyst may have contact only with a committee comprising councillors, or heads of academic departments, or managers of certain departments which use the library service. These will not be the people who are actively engaged in the day to day running of the library system.

7

collecting data about the system

Once the preliminary steps have been taken the analyst is ready to plan the way in which the data will be collected. There are three methods of collection, and the choice will be governed as much by the availability of staff to undertake the work involved, as by the accessibility of the various parts of the organisation to be investigated. In most situations the survey is conducted by a mixture of all three methods, since this way lends itself to a more balanced view of the existing system. The three methods are: interview, questionnaire, observation.

INTERVIEW

Those who have already attempted to conduct interviews eliciting information about people's work will know that the whole exercise is fraught with difficulty. Each interview is different and there is nothing to be gained from trying to confine these to a single form. The questioners certainly will have an interview sheet on which are reminders of the points which need to be covered, the remainder of the sheet being used to make notes as the talk progresses. Textbooks on the subject rightly emphasise the need for putting interviewees at their ease in comfortable and at least semi-private conditions. One never knows just what will come out of these meetings and it is essential to avoid stifling anything important through lack of privacy. Few people will discuss their job in the sort of detail which the analyst needs and it will be for him to guide the conversation as unobtrusively and unobstructively as possible. This may mean that the envisaged plan for an interview may not be adhered to, and that the result will have to be written up afterwards. In this connection it is customary to make brief notes only, since an interviewer who appears to be writing down every word will cause considerable suspicion about his motives. A good interview is conducted in a relaxed and informal way, allowing the maximum of confidence and encouraging suggestion or comment where appropriate. There are some textbooks which have hinted that suggestions, however impractical, should be received with approbation. Such patronising is to be deplored and leads to quite ludicrous results, since workers are quick to sense such artificial situations and may be excused for baiting the interviewer with increasingly extravagant suggestions. Most people are proud of the way they execute their work, at whatever level, and it is therefore vital to ensure that at no time is there any suggestion that the interviewer regards the work being discussed as menial. The other factor to be guarded against is the glorious hobby horse which gets leapt on to at the first opportunity. To persuade people down from these, or indeed to recognise them quickly, is an art which the good interviewer cultivates early in his career. In some situations there may also be the temptation to treat complaints without very much seriousness. However, it is only when the data are collated and analysed that the weight of any given complaint can be assessed and it may well transpire that discontent is rife in connection with certain operations within the organisation. Such matters have to be given due consideration when designing the new system.

The matter of when such interviews should be held is also an important question. It is well known that ill chosen times, such as when the person to be questioned is exceptionally busy, or likely to be much fatigued after a peak work load, or worse, due to go home or break for lunch, can all result in unsatisfactory interviews. All these will obviously predispose the subject to be less concerned about the outcome of the interview and keen to end it quickly. Lastly it should be said that not every interview will provide that satisfactory relationship which gains confidences and gets people talking. An interviewer has to be prepared to accept that sometimes only a formal confrontation is achieved. But even this can tell him a lot when the data are married up with those from other more successful sessions.

QUESTIONNAIRES

Much has already been written about the design of questionnaires, and it is not the intention here to cover the ground yet again. We will content ourselves with observing that as you ask so will they answer. This means that questions must be clear, easily answered and provide for as many approaches as could reasonably be expected. If the results are to be collated for statistical analysis, they need to be structured in a way allowing collation to be carried out with the minimum of effort. It is thus necessary to number each question and the answers, all of which should be closed wherever possible. In the case of open questions, where the respondent is allowed to answer in his own words, codes can be allotted according to the various categories of answer which transpire. Three things are certain about the success of questionnaires. Firstly, they must be of an acceptable length, otherwise the latter part will be almost useless. Secondly, cross checks must be incorporated into the questionnaire to guard against the respondent merely providing answers which he feels will gain approval. Finally, the anonymity of respondents should be seen to be preserved, otherwise answers will be less than frank.

OBSERVATION

It has now become common knowledge that workers who are watched performing their tasks will often alter their behaviour pattern or 'put on a show'. This is a mere human reaction arising as much from a wish to present oneself in the best possible light, as a certain self-consciousness which may impair performance. With these considerations in mind, it is quite possible to get firsthand information from workers while actually on the job. This is much better done after the interviews which give an opportunity for extracting agreement to visit the scene of operations. With the right approach there is no reason at all why such methods of gaining data about work flow, times and responsibilities should not prove acceptable to the staff in general and useful to the analyst. While noting the sequence of operations associated with a job, the analyst will also be able to discover the various documents and forms which are used and wherever possible he will take samples away for reference.

Having chosen the methods of data collection, it will then be necessary to design the forms and questionnaires which are to be used. It is normal to undertake a small pilot study to determine the suitability of the forms, which are then altered in the light of this experience. Once the matter has been settled there is the need to decide on the amount of labour which will be required to carry out some of the survey work. In some cases the time scale of the whole analysis is such that the analyst can afford to do all the work himself, only recruiting help for the collation and analysis of the data. In library situations it would not be unusual for library students or selected members of the staff to be used to examine reader habits, library use, and so on. If such personnel are to be used it may be necessary to devise a handout giving details of the way in which certain jobs must be executed and recorded. For good measure the analyst should brief them before work is begun.

CHARTING PROCEDURES

A visit to departmental heads will provide a general outline of what operations occur within each, and who is responsible for each stage. This provides an indication of the way in which the work flows and the type of documents involved. From such information it is possible to construct an outline flow-chart similar to the one in FIGURE 14, which shows the structure for a large lending department in a public library.

The next task is to chart the various procedures as they occur. This means recording what the analyst sees happen in a way which allows him later to know the status of each operation and the time required to complete it. Since there will be a lot of this kind of information it is sensible to standardise the way in which it is presented. Many use the symbols of ASME (American Society of Mechanical Engineers) as illustrated in FIGURE 15. When recording the stages of a procedure one can either use a linear display or a flowchart. The difference between the two is illustrated in FIGURES 16 and 17, which show the reservation procedure. During these sessions, the analyst will be wanting copies of all forms used, and he will require a number of these, preferably completed in the normal way. This is an important point since often forms, ostensibly designed for a particular use, prove unsuitable in one or two respects, so that there are sections permanently unused whilst information, not allowed for at the time of their design, has to be added in wherever space is available. These deficiencies will not come to light if merely unused forms are taken as samples.

The purpose of examining the procedures at every level is to answer the following questions:

What is achieved at each stage of a procedure?
In what order do they occur?
Who carries out each part of the procedure?
How long does each stage take?
What volume of work, items, etc is involved?
Why is the procedure or its stages necessary?

All the time the analyst must keep an open mind about all that he sees and discovers. Accept nothing as being inherently valuable or necessary until it has been assessed objectively and critically. The age-old reply of 'We have always done it this way' is to be challenged ruthlessly so that a new system will incorporate only those features of the old which have proven worth. With this in mind, the work of analysis will progress until all the appropriate parts of the organisation have been examined in sufficient detail to provide the data from which the new system will be designed.

When the data are collated and analysed, there should be a clear picture of the flow and volume of work, documents and information. From such data it should also be possible to identify those parts of the present system which may be changed, together with those which must be incorporated in any new system. For instance, while it may transpire that the loans system may be changed radically, providing the required control is maintained, the method of cataloguing may not be amenable to any change at all. This is not to say that the appropriate questions should not be asked about the cataloguing methods, but that the answers provided make it quite clear that current practice is adequate.

8
stages of systems design

With the analysis complete, the analyst is now ready to begin tentative designs for a new system. The order in which he approaches the whole operation has implications for the success of the scheme, and if the order is wrong he may find that some parts of the system prove inadequate. We shall therefore consider the stages of design in the order which the analyst should be expected to take them.

OUTPUT

Although earlier meetings with the management will have elicited some expectations concerning desired outputs, the analysis will have thrown up a number of possibilities which may not have been foreseen. These should be clarified and discussed further with the management to ascertain their economic acceptability. Thus, for example, the claim that analysis had revealed that an on-line service should be provided at two or three key points may be legitimate, but nevertheless unacceptable. Similarly, the analyst may conclude that the equivalent of a catalogue should be made available at many more points and that this would be best achieved by the use of microforms. However, early consultation with the management may establish that they would be unwilling to vote the money required for special readers. Obviously that which is to be derived from a system will govern the design. It is therefore a prerequisite to finalise, with general approval, the output from the new system. Having started on the output, the designer works backwards through the system so that sectors which are dependent are designed before those on which they depend.

DATA BASE

Once we know what is wanted from the system, the data base content can be specified. In the library situation it is possible to have a complete or abbreviated catalogue entry as the record on which system activity will depend. Obviously the choice will affect the amount of information available and the type of interrogation possible. If continual listing of file content are required, the data base may have to provide files in various orders, the alternative being to sort and resort before each listing. It may also be decided that one record will not meet all requirements and that various files will be provided for different purposes.

INPUTS

Having specified the file content, we then have to devise methods of entering the necessary data. This involves deciding not only the frequency at which data is to be entered on file, but also the way in which it is to be fed in. The choice will often be dictated by circumstances, but may initially be between the use of a terminal connected on-line to the computer, or off-line using punched cards or the like, which are taken to the computer section for processing.

FORM DESIGN

All the data to be generated throughout the system, and which are required for input to the files, will have to be controlled. This means the provision of suitable forms on which relevant information can be recorded having due regard to the input methods. The layout of these forms affects the efficient translation of the data they carry into acceptable input format. At the same time such forms can arise as part of the output from the system. So not only must the forms accept all the required information, but also be of a size convenient for handling. There is also the matter of the number of copies of each form required. The layout will also reflect the route which the form takes through the system to acquire the necessary entries, and it will recognise the need for the form to be filed at various points. Such designs have to be acceptable to both users and management.

WORK FLOW AND DISTRIBUTION

The new way in which the work progresses through the organisation will obviously be structured to promote maximum efficiency. Also at this point will be decided which personnel are to do what, whether singly or in groups, and the work load allocated to each sector.

PROCESSING

Knowing the outputs, inputs and the flow of data we are now in a position to decide on the processing which can take place. The analyst will specify how the data is to be treated and how often. The particular point at issue here is the amount of processing which will be allocated to the computer. Obviously the less required to be done manually the better, but this entails relinquishing immediate control so that continual checks may be necessary or that the many exceptions give rise to uneconomic operation. There is a balance which may only be achieved in the light of experience gained with the new system.

PROGRAM SPECIFICATIONS

To achieve the required processing the computer has to have programs. Some of these, such as sort routines, may be available as part of the standard computer software. For the more specialised applications there may be packages which contain a suite of programs to execute certain jobs connected with one type of data. Thus the MARC program suites which should soon be available for those wishing to base their systems on MARC type bibliographic records, should obviate the need to write many programs for local requirements. The analyst will outline in a general way the processing required and programmers will then assemble, adapt or generate the necessary software to suit the system.

IMPLEMENTATION

Many libraries have found that it is neither convenient nor wise to attempt conversion of the entire library system to a computer based one. It is therefore usual practice to begin with the area which will give the most benefit or, equally popular, that area which is most amenable to conversion (usually the loans system). Whatever is decided upon, the analyst will be called upon to give some time scale for the total conversion. This enables those responsible to work towards realistic goals and to forecast the cost at any stage.

SYSTEM FLEXIBILITY

Each analyst recognises that he is unlikely to have thought of every possible development which may occur within the system he has designed. It is therefore customary to ensure that the system can be altered to suit an expanding organisation or to handle data in different ways. Such changes as can be foreseen will be outlined and possible ways of meeting them examined.

COSTS

It is only at this stage that the overall costs can be reckoned. Management will want to know the capital cost of conversion to the new system and the running costs for given throughputs. Here consideration would be given to the merits of using outside agencies for certain jobs, of accepting data generated by an outside organisation, and so on. Such costs must also include those which might be incurred over new stationery, equipment, or personnel. More important perhaps, will be the savings which such a system might be expected to achieve. However, it should be stressed that often a library is not compelled to accept a system on the grounds of the economies it can provide. For example, the maintenance of a vast catalogue may be proved quite uneconomic, but library policy may make its provision mandatory. Likewise a system which is required to give high recall must necessarily be expensive and wasteful, but if this is deemed of paramount importance one looks for a design which achieves the least wastage.

DOCUMENTATION

All the way through the designing, the analyst will have been recording the features of each part of the system, the way in which they interrelate, and the documents associated with each. It is this documentation which becomes vitally important when the analyst has long since gone and parts of the system begin to show the need for reappraisal. It explains the system to all who have a need to know. It will also specify the deadline for any suggestions for modifications or additions to the system, after which the system will be allowed to work without any interference for a period usually of about nine months. Thereafter it will be possible to introduce other alterations.

This breathing space is very necessary to allow a realistic assessment to be made of the suitability of the design.

The above ten stages have been briefly annotated to give some indication of the work to be done at the design stage. However, there may be some readers who feel they would like further knowledge of the more important stages. The next part of this book presents various aspects of input, processing and output.

9
input procedures

Just as a library will standardise its catalogue entries in order to promote accuracy, uniformity of practice and ease of use, so do the input procedures of a mechanised system need to be standardised as much as possible. There are other benefits to be derived from such action in that errors are more easily detected and the speed of processing is much assisted. However, the method evolved will depend initially on whether the bibliographic data is to be encoded by library staff or by professional punch operators. It should be stressed here that while both situations permit some flexibility, the professional punch operator is trained to depress keys at rates exceeding 8,000 per hour, so it is not normal practice for her to check data before punching it out. This means in effect that the operator will encode exactly what she sees before her—mistakes as well. Often those using punching services are surprised, if not pained, to find all their own errors faithfully reproduced. The moral is that if encoding is to be done correctly then the system must be designed to provide the information in a way which is quick to read and easily checked.

Once the matter of who is going to do the encoding has been resolved, we can then decide on the appropriate way in which original data will be presented for encoding. Obviously the less writing to be done the better; cataloguing from source can offer appreciable savings in this connection.

There are thus two methods of data presentation: *a*) use of originals with annotations; *b*) use of punching sheet. For the present we are ignoring the possible use of optical character or other special readers since it would still be necessary to provide an entry which could be fed into the reader, which brings us back to the equivalent of the two options given. In the case of the first it is obvious that staff belonging to, or giving a considerable amount of cooperation to, the library would be required to do the encoding. Information is taken direct from publications with further information added in the appropriate or agreed places by whoever is responsible for the compilation of entries for inclusion in the system. This reduces transcription before encoding to a minimum. It must surely be obvious that the variety of ways in which the required entry data may be presented could prove troublesome for any but those familiar with library practice. It is precisely because this way of working may not be possible that the second method may have to be used. In this case the data relating to one entry is written out on a form which is then passed to the punch operator for encoding. Such a form needs to be arranged to afford a fixed place for every possible data element in an entry and at the same time assist the punch operator to work quickly and accurately.

Whatever is input has to be amenable to change, and it is essential that additions and amendments can be effected as part of the regular procedures and not as exceptions. It is therefore sensible to provide punching sheets both for setting up a record as well as for altering it. In the latter case it would be necessary to provide an indicator showing that the data relate to a record already on file. Such alterations would be allowed for in the programs but this assumes careful planning. What has to be avoided is the need to alter programs substantially.

A word here about accuracy. In manual files we are used to the situation where if a mistake is discovered it can then be corrected almost on the spot. With computer files this of course is not the case. What is more, making changes in computer files is certainly more costly than manual files. It is therefore worthwhile to strive after a high degree of accuracy so that the number of changes are kept down and the files kept reliable. Depending on the way in which the system operates, those wanting information from the files may actually interrogate them on the computer (rather than scan a complete printout of their contents), which means that inaccuracies in their content will prevent relevant items being produced against such interrogation. It must also be recognised that as the files grow, so the possibility of printing out their contents becomes less and less attractive, a prospect facing cumulative files.

To return to the form, take a look at the one illustrated in FIGURE 18. One feature common to all such sheets is the requirement for all data to be written in capitals, in this instance one character per box, and that spaces are indicated clearly by b̸ or ▽. The letter 'O' is distinguished from nought by one having a stroke through it. Such devices most easily avoid mistakes. As can be seen, the form reflects the layout of the data on punched cards or paper tape, so that there is a clear indication of where each data element starts. When using punched cards, each line of the punching sheet could be coded onto a separate card. With paper tape, however, an end-of-field sign would have to be inserted between each data element irrespective of its length. Obviously the arrangement is made to suit each system, but if continual changes are to be avoided it is essential to allow for most contingencies, even if some elements may not be introduced until the system has been running some time or will be wanted only occasionally. This is much better than having to add headings in as things progress. This is not to say that the punching sheet is unchangeable, but new layouts can slow the procedure for a while. It is also usual to use different punching sheets according to purpose, *eg* amendments or deletions, as illustrated in FIGURE 19.

Once entries have been encoded they will need to be checked for transcription errors. In the case of punched cards there will not usually be any printed copy of what has been punched. There are some machines which permit the automatic production via a typewriter of a printed version of the characters punched into the cards. Conventional card punches may incorporate a special printing device, which prints the character above the column into which it has been punched. Cards having a readable version of the punched data displayed along the top are said to be *interpreted*. Where punches do not have a printing device, it is possible to feed the punched cards through another machine called an interpreter, which will print onto the card the characters in each column.

Assuming, therefore, that the punching sheets are correct (which means that they should be thoroughly checked before submission), the punched cards (or punched paper tape) may be handed over to another operator who will verify them. This process requires that a different operator goes through the motions of encoding all the data again using the same punching documents and same punched cards or tape. However, the verifying machine does not record the keying, but checks each key depression against what has been previously punched. Where the character keyed in and that already punched fail to match, the machine signals the fact. The operator is then given a second chance to check the character. A repeat failure to match, in the case of cards, will mean the card containing the fault is rejected with some indicator like a notch at the bottom of the column in which the wrong character occurs. In the case of paper tape verification, a duplicate tape is generated from that punched out first, and where mistakes (*ie* unmatched characters) are detected the correct character is punched into the duplicate tape.

Where tape-typewriters are used, there will also be a printed copy which could be used to check against. Verifying can also be done where magnetic tape encoders are used, but in this case there is nothing readable available for checking until the tape has been run through the computer.

In the case of on-line input where a terminal is connected to the computer, it is possible to input data as they are encoded. In the case of a typewriter terminal the hard copy produced at the terminal at the time of keying in the data can be used for checking the accuracy of the data. In the case of the visual display unit, it is possible to have encoded data immediately displayed on the screen. To maintain input speeds at economical levels such checking might be more satisfactorily done at intervals, leaving corrections to be effected later on. Although on-line input has considerable attractions since the main file is kept current and special runs for updating are not required (though this depends on the way the system is designed), there are also problems. Unless the person using the terminal is very proficient, the time required to input say 10,000 characters might be quite uneconomic. This in turn could mean that the terminal would have to be operating for longer periods than the total computer system might permit during working hours. It would therefore be more economic to prepare a paper tape locally and transmit the 10,000 characters in a block over the terminal. It is assumed here that the library would be sharing the on-line facilities with others having terminals operating during the day.

RECORD CONTENT

Having said that input data should comprise all that is ever likely to be required by the demands made on the system, the question still remains as to just what that might be. One might for instance decide to include every element provided in a MARC record (discussed later). For many libraries this would be more than is necessary. Yet to use the content as given in many catalogues might well prove insufficient. During the discussion on systems design, mention was made of the need to look at every mechanisation project as a total systems concept to ensure integration and satisfactory interdependence. Record content must be determined in the light of what the system is expected to provide. The entry in FIGURE 20 shows a number of familiar elements which one might expect to see allowed for on a punching sheet. As can be seen, not all the items shown would be present in every record. Thus an order's record will have minimum bibliographic information, but will include details about supplier, date of ordering, number of copies, expected distribution and funds against which the costs are to be charged. A full catalogue entry would presumably have minimal, if any, ordering information. It must be apparent that the decision about the content of records is governed by the requirements of each system. There is no merit in attempting to arrive at one all purpose record for use with every local system. A system, though, can benefit enormously from the use of a single record format to serve all purposes within the system.

One of the cries of computer enthusiasts concerns high speeds and capacities of storage devices (both of which are increasing every year). Does this mean that we can discount any thoughts of economy in record content? If we take the average record provided on a BNB/MARC tape as typical of library records, we can reckon on their length being about 1,000 characters (at the time of writing). Therefore a standard reel of magnetic tape of 2,400 feet with a density of 800 cpi (characters per inch) would accept 14,400 records, allowing for inter-block gaps (a block here equals one record). If exchangeable disc packs are used with a capacity of 22 million characters, approximately 20,000 records could be stored. The cumulation of such files demands considerable thought about any economies which might be effected to save not only space but probably processing times as well. Storage on discs is expensive, while tapes are cheap enough but have not the capacity, so that large files can extend over a considerable number of them. With this in mind, there must arise the conflict between completeness and utility. It is a temptation to start a system being much too generous and end up searching for elements to delete as the pressure for file space grows. This is not to suggest that records cannot satisfactorily contain all that is desirable, but that every element should be justified.

10
the record

FORMAT

Before discussing record format in general, it may be helpful to explain what is meant by 'fixed' and 'variable' fields. If you look at FIGURE 21 it can be seen that a certain number of columns or characters have been allotted to each data element or field. Not only is the number of characters fixed but the position of each field in relation to others may not be changed. There is one variation possible, however, and that relates to the number of characters which actually appear in each such field. The accession number might always be the same length, but author's names would obviously vary in length. In the case of variable fields, the number of characters which may be required in each field is unpredictable and therefore without restriction. So in the case of a fixed field, unless the data element is always of the same length, such an element will often be too long or too short to fit the field provided. With the former the field content has to be truncated, while with the latter unused character places are wasted. Neither of these situations would be acceptable for bibliographic files. It is for this reason that the variable field format is to be preferred. It permits a field to be as long as the data in it when the amount of data can vary unpredictably.

It is necessary to indicate the end of each variable field, as well as the end of the entire record by unique characters, that is, used for this purpose only when occurring by themselves or with other predictable characters. In the case of card input, data elements can be punched on separate cards so that the author's name appears on the first, the title on the next (abbreviated if necessary) and so on (FIGURE 22), or the data can be punched on in one sequence on as many cards as required (FIGURE 23). With paper tape there need be no wastage, since there is little to be gained by leaving spaces between elements or records, and the program can format the data into fixed fields. In either case there is good reason for keeping down the number of cards or the amount of tape to be fed into the computer. Reading or input rates are dependent on the physical speed with which cards or tape can pass through the reader.

The two formats are not mutually exclusive, however. The choice hinges on the intended use to which the file will be put. Certainly the quickest system will use fixed field whether serial or direct access systems are used. But since bibliographic data elements are notoriously unpredictable in length, fixed fields for every element would have to be wastefully long to cater for an unknown number of lengthy exceptions. A further point to be remembered is that the same data element may not be present in every record which, in the case of fixed field format, would mean unused areas. Such a wasteful practice is quite unacceptable in the size of files associated with libraries. The first consideration on formatting is the way in which every record is to be uniquely identified. Certainly a number is to be preferred to an alphabetic or mixed code. No doubt as its use grows the International Standard Book Numbering (ISBN) system will serve enough. For those items without such a number, a local one can be generated which has the same format but is obviously different. Since this number is to be used to call up a record, its physical location in the record should be at the front, so that the first set of characters always contains this number. Following this, there can be a variety of elements, but if they are to be frequently used as search parameters these ought to be of fixed length. It should perhaps be explained that variable field data can also be searched, but not so easily. The search program can reach an element in fixed field format by counting the characters in sets until the correct character places are found, then the characters themselves are compared for an exact match with those in the search. In the case of variable field format an element is reached either through the equivalent of an index to the record content, or checking character by character for a match. Each variable field may be identified by its relative position to the others, thus the author would always be the first data element in the record. Unfortunately there may not always be an author so this method may not be adequate. However, it would be possible to insert a blank space followed by a field terminator wherever an element is missing. This would mean that in cases where there were, for example, a maximum of sixty fields, the same number of terminators would always have to be present in each record. Any attempt to introduce more fields within the sixty would require the reformating of every record already on file. This is necessary because the position of every element in the sequence must be the same in every record using this system. It is therefore preferable to code each element uniquely. This code would precede the data to which it relates, so that a fixed number of characters at the beginning of each field will always be used for this purpose. The code used is entirely arbitrary, but must cater for the maximum number of fields and provide aids to searching.

MARC (*MAchine Readable Catalogue*)

The MARC project was begun by the Library of Congress in 1965 as an attempt to provide bibliographic data in machine readable form for items being received. The present MARC II format was developed in 1967 and published a year later. This was based on a much broader intention than the original scheme, since by 1967 it had become plain that much could be gained from a format which could be used for the transfer of data between bibliographic centres.

Let us now look at the way in which the MARC II format meets the criteria given above. The illustration in FIGURE 24 shows elements grouped according to function. The numbers are structured to assist in identifying the elements within each group. Thus a main entry heading element will have a number beginning 1 . . , title beginning 2 . . , while annotations and the like begin 5 . . . It will also be noticed that where a corporate name occurs, whatever its function, the group number will always be followed by .10 with the exception of group 0 and of course the unallocated group 9.

Although the list of fields is considerable, it is not expected that any organisation would want to use them all. It is for this reason the MARC is to be regarded as a format for the exchange of bibliographic data rather than a catalogue, this latter arising only after the library using MARC has processed the records for its own use, by editing out unwanted fields. Looking at the illustration of a MARC record in FIGURE 25, we can see the first part—the leader—is fixed field showing the length of the record (required for machine purposes) and then its status, etc; thus N=New, A=Printed matter, M=Monograph, etc. The record directory is that strange mixture 'fixed variable field', since each group of figures have 12 numbers, but there will be as many groups as there are fields in the data part of the record. Following the directory is more fixed field information about the record such as the ISBN, date of entry on the file, date of publication, and so on. Finally come the data fields themselves which must be variable in length. In this example the plus sign indicates the end of a field (a field terminator), while 00£A begins each variable field. It can be seen that the title of the work is split up, parts (sub-fields) being prefixed by £M, £L and £K. (The letters used in this case for sub-fields also have significance for processing.) This device enables a search to be made for elements which may form a part of any field.

As has been explained all the jobs carried out on a computer require a program. A change in the job specification in turn requires a change to be made in the program. To do this to some programs is not difficult, but where a highly complex program is used any change may well equal the task and trouble of producing a new program and there may also be the necessity to reformat the records. To change one's mind about record structure is therefore a matter of caution. Take, for example, the title as given in FIGURE 25. Could one extract the information prefixed by £M and £L without these signs? Obviously as part of the title they must appear in the field, and therefore if the whole field is extracted that data will also be taken out. But it is not possible automatically to separate out similar sub-field information from every record without indicators. In this example, were the sub-field indicators not there, it would not be possible to make a list automatically of all conferences by place and number. Without some instruction to the computer by which it can recognise the relevant part of the title, there is no way of indicating what is to be used as the *sort key* (explained later) in this case.

DATA COMPACTION

As mentioned under record content, there is no limit to the amount of data which may be included in a record. Certainly the limitations of any machine used should not be allowed to radically curtail the information desirable in such records. Nevertheless, there is the need to look closely at the potentialities of any mechanised system and the way in which modifications to original intentions for the system may exploit those potentialities. Obviously the machine should not be allowed to dictate the system design, nor should the existing manual system be regarded as the model. In this light one may look at the matter of record size. The larger the data base, that is the greater the number of records to be included, the longer are the search times and the more expensive the storage. It is therefore in the interests of economy and speed that every means is explored for compacting records. Some of these, being machine based and the responsibility of the programmer, will not be discussed here. Other ways of compacting concern the way in which the data are offered. It should be emphasised that the omission of even one character in every record can show appreciable savings. If it were agreed to omit the article occurring at the front of many titles, the average saving in a file of 50,000 records might be reckoned at 100,000 characters, which in turn means room for up to 100 additional records. The traditional view of such practices may well be too strong for some to accept such economies, but when making such concessions to mechanisation the resulting benefits should be borne in mind. Other economies of this kind are also possible without any significant reduction in efficiency. Thus the place of publication may be abbreviated when well known, and similarly the publisher can often be reduced to initials, as can the titles of periodicals, providing that such abbreviations are in accordance with some generally accepted system. In the case of periodicals this might be the code devised by the American Society for Testing and Materials—CODEN (FIGURE 26), but this uses only five characters and could prove too brief for easy recognition despite offering very favourable machine search facilities. One complaint which might be made about such methods is that although they suit machine manipulation, they are not particularly pleasant to the eye when printed out in bibliographies. It is this very point which needs careful thought before finalising the system design. Just how often is full information required in the library? So many enquiries are satisfied by information sufficient to identify or locate the work, the bibilographic detail necessary to meet this requirement being quite brief. We are talking here at the local level, of course, since data intended for the use of a large variety of libraries could not be abbreviated without impairing the value. Once passed to the local user, though, there is no reason why records cannot be automatically edited and acceptable abbreviations substituted.

There cannot be any doubt that a system which uses data in this form would be quite unacceptable if all such abbreviations had to be provided manually. It is an essential feature of such systems that programs are written which edit the data as part of the input run. It should also be part of such systems that the output run includes an option for printing out abbreviated elements in full. This assumes that such an option would be used only occasionally, since frequent use of it would add to output running times and thereby defeat any savings made by using abbreviations in the first place.

11
processing

For many libraries the question does not arise of whether to operate the system on a continuous basis or by batching. Computer facilities are made available to the library without particular regard to its needs, and it has to make use of what is left after those with higher priorities have made their claims. Batch processing can be done with both off-line and on-line facilities. Much will depend on the volume of work to be done and the number of staff. But whatever considerations determine the way in which the system will operate, the ability to keep up to date with on-line files offers many advantages. However, quite apart from the cost of the terminals needed, and the processor and storage devices necessary to hold large files on direct access, there are practical considerations which discourage wide use. Even with the large third generation computers, store size still appreciably limits the number of users who can be served at the same time. A library system which was wholly mechanised could monopolise the computer at peak periods, a situation unlikely to be tolerated for long by other users. A further point is that teleprinter terminals are noisy and not particularly fast (speeds average about 30 characters a second) while visual display units although fast and noiseless do not produce printed copy. Lastly, where a number of departments have terminals it is normal practice to determine a priority rating. Under this scheme terminals with a high priority can obtain access to the store almost immediately, which in turn means that lower priority users experience some delay. Although such delays are not likely to be more than three minutes, these could be rather disruptive during busy periods.

However, looking at the two ways of processing, it can be seen that batching allows the amount of data to be accumulated, so that the computer's time is given entirely to processing. Presented with a large amount of input data to encode, for instance, the operator can reach maximum speed, thus making for maximum efficiency. Batching must also be carried out at frequent intervals if the files are to remain up to date. Thus if the updating run, accepting new data for the files, making any amendments necessary and producing whatever output is wanted, was made only once a week, it would be necessary to have manual files for the inter-run period. But batching need not be as infrequent as this, and it is certain that as libraries become regular users their demands for computer time will be more readily met. Daily data processing would probably suit most libraries, though in some cases even this time lag may be unacceptable. The chief consideration in batch processing is that computer time is used efficiently.

Librarians often find that time on the computer is not fully costed out to the library which results in less incentive to be concerned about economies. It is not merely the cost which should govern the way in which a system operates but also the turnround time. This is the speed at which the whole processing cycle is completed. Note that the cycle consists of the input, processing, output and delivery of any documentation arising from the run. This in effect means that where a computer installation is at a distance from the user, the turnround time will include travelling and transport time. The time on the computer may be only twenty minutes, but if the van calls only once a day the turnround time is twenty four hours. In the case of batching, the running speeds are kept at their maximum. The efficiency of continuous processing, as would occur with an on-line system, depends entirely on the way in which the work flows and the speed of the terminal operator. If the operator has continually to wait until more work arrives, or worse, to edit input data while the terminal is live, computer time is obviously not being used efficiently. Besides the provision of a trained operator for the terminal, there is one other way in which even the less proficient can make sensible use of on-line facilities. This relies on the terminal having a paper tape punch and reading head. The terminal is used to generate data onto the paper tape but not in the real-time mode, *ie* without having the line to the computer live at the time the data are encoded. This method is known as off-line. When there are sufficient data to make it worthwhile, the terminal is switched on and the paper tape fed through at a higher speed than manual input. Thus it is quite possible to have an on-line system which nevertheless operates in a batch mode.

What happens to data once they have been fed into the computer? Obviously they are then processed in some way so that each record is held in such a format as to permit recall against any number of acceptable parameters. The program used for accepting data to be included in the file will at the same time carry out various operations. Reverting to our example of a MARC record, it would be quite intolerable if the directory had to be constructed and fed into the computer. It is the work of the programmer to ensure that every task possible is made an automatic part of a process run. There are many such operations performed in this way, most being needed by the machine rather than the users of the system. However, certain record structuring operations directly relate to the parameters which users have asked to be made available. It will often be necessary to extract records relating to the same author, subject, or organisation. In other words these may be used as search parameters and must be recoverable against every record containing them. We have seen how this might be achieved using a MARC structure. But even by this method it would be necessary to search every record via each directory to get at such information. Searching every record is a fast enough matter with high speed computers, but where the data base is large, the search times would still be too great. It must be remembered that many such systems are quite fairly measured against the time taken for an equivalent manual system. If one has to talk about search times of the order of thirty minutes, when consulting a catalogue takes five, users are rightly unimpressed. It is thus necessary to arrange records in various orders to meet differing needs. To gain such order each record has to have a 'sort key' as the first set of characters. This is used by the sort programs to determine the sequence of the records. The key can be automatically generated from the data given in the body of the record, providing of course that such data have been tagged.

Earlier it was stated that the processing run may be expected to perform several various functions. It is, in fact, economical to have as many jobs as possible done as part of the same run. It is usual with every computer installation that use is scheduled to run given jobs at roughly agreed times. The frequency of a job is initially estimated, and after a few runs given a time slot. Such a slot will be allocated to that run and will be expected to last for an estimated time. This makes difficult the addition of further jobs to a scheduled regular run. Although extended jobs may be run, the pressure of work to be executed for other users may mean that extra jobs have to be deferred until a slack period. Some computer managers prefer to have many short jobs, which would allow the use of a number of smaller programs, although the large complex one can also be used.

While on the subject of scheduled runs, there arises the matter of data tapes (magnetic tapes containing data for processing) which are generated outside the organisation. Such would be MARC tapes supplied by BNB every week. If the processing run is scheduled for a given time each weekday, failure to arrive on time may mean postponement of the run until the next scheduled run. Not all computer installations are operated twenty four hours a day, so the often quiet night shift may not be available for picking up outstanding jobs.

SEARCH REQUIREMENTS

The structure of the files and the format of the records must enable them to match the requirements of the system users. Thus it should be possible to interrogate the file using any combination of parameters. These may be defined as data elements which form the whole or part of a field, or identifiers contained within the record. The ideal system will permit the use of any number of these parameters in a search. The search formulation (discussed later) is made by listing the parameters required to be present in a record to establish a match. Such a list is called a *search profile* in just the same way as the indexing data relating to a document forms the document profile, while personal profiles list an individual's interests, and can be compared against each set of new records as they become available.

Records subjected to such interrogation will obviously have the potential to afford matches where appropriate. This does not mean that the maximum possible data must be present, but that the data base comprises such elements as the system design intended. Any limitations which emerge at the search stage are the result of design decisions. The comprehensive record offers the maximum facility, while brief records, which might be associated with ordering or loans, would naturally be a less flexible base. In the case of a full catalogue entry, the MARC type record format would enable a search to be made for a considerable variety of elements. Thus: first or other authors, whole or parts of titles (as with conferences), etc. Used in combination, bibliographies can be compiled for works by a given author during a certain period or in a certain format (*eg* plays, novels, non-fiction), or on a given subject published during a certain period and in certain countries. But not all searches are so clear cut. Where different combinations from the same set of parameters would give an acceptable match, that is, the item so retrieved would be deemed relevant to the enquiry, there should be the facility to formulate a search in this way. Since information retrieval associated with bibliographical files is a subject for separate treatment, it is not intended to expand on it here. Suffice to say that search statements can be as simple or as complex as the programs permit.

Anyone used to handling bibliographies will be wondering how the machine is able to cope with authors when misspelt by the searcher. In the manual situation we can compensate for such errors by making adjustments to our search procedure as it progresses. By such means we are able to detect near matches which when coupled with other parameters like subject matter often enable appropriate selection to be made. The computer, however, as every instructor is at pains to emphasise, does not parallel our behaviour in error situations. No rationalisation process is set in motion, and therefore either the program has to cater for such situations or the computer will endeavour to make a match with the wrongly spelt author. This may result in a false match or failure to match at all. A provision in the program for the possibility of misspellings would entail far too much checking, making search times inordinately long. There are really only two options available. The first is that authors must be checked in appropriate sources before submitting for a search, or there must be an acceptance of some failure in matching. This latter, of course, does itself act as an alerting system, in that the non-match can suggest an error as well as the genuine absence of relevant items in the file. There have been some experiments (Dolby, 1971) made on ways in which words might be compressed to permit matching even when misspelt.

The uses to which a bibliographic file can be put ultimately rest with the programs available. Every computer manufacturer offers software for running various standard type jobs. It is possible therefore to obtain programs already written by the manufacturers or indeed by firms specialising in this service to do some of the jobs. However, these ' package ' programs demand that the data processed by them are presented a certain way, and permit handling the data only in accordance with the package dictates. Therefore the system has to fit the package or it cannot be used. The attraction about these is that they are tested and proved, and require little or no work on them before use. What is more, their capabilities are known and so expectations can be realistic. However, those very capabilities may also be an undesirable limitation to the expansive design. Quite often the hopeful package user discovers that alterations which become desirable in the light of system growth may be impossible (programs are usually supplied already compiled), while the limitations become increasingly irksome. For this reason many users prefer to commission their own programs. The decision facing one here is whether to require that the program carries out certain jobs with conditions given, or whether the program is generalised so that the conditions are specified at each run. By conditions we mean the state of the data submitted for processing and the way in which this dictates the action to be taken during the run. In a specialised program one might find such conditions as: if the Dewey class number of the work to be entered on file lies between 620 and 669, notify via the printer; if the work to which the submitted data refers is on loan to any of the following numbers (a list of special borrower numbers would then be given) ignore it. Where such conditions are unlikely to change, there is no objection to putting them in as part of the program. But for many situations, especially in the early stages of using a program, the need to change these conditions may arise unexpectedly often. If they have been incorporated in the program, any changes which become necessary may involve retesting before using. If the conditions are outside the program, the changes in any set may be effected by submitting them on cards or paper tape at the beginning of the run. Thus in the case of special borrowers, the numbers can be changed if a new set is submitted at the beginning of each run as part of the input. This latter gives a much more flexible system but entails considerably more programming effort at the expense of programming efficiency. The great advantage of using generalised programs lies in the facility to vary the system design somewhat.

THE DATA BASE

Although one talks about the data base as though it were just one file, a system need not be restricted in this way. There may be very good reasons for keeping a number of files in operation which are used for different jobs. Thus there may be a file for controlling loans, another for dealing with serials receipts and another for items on order. These are essentially the commercial equivalent of active files in that the data in them are constantly being changed and their size remains fairly constant. But it does also mean that in the case of libraries similar data appear in more than one place in the system. To avoid such duplication it is possible to provide a single file which allows all information relating to an item to be located in one record. By such an arrangement the entire status and detail of an item can be made available with the search of one file only.

Quite obviously in the situation where a number of files are used, each record can be kept smaller than is the case where use is made of just one file. As a consequence such records relating to loans, for example, can be structured in fixed field format to allow fast processing. There is a further possible benefit to be derived from this arrangement, in that since the file, being active, remains fairly constant in size, it is not too great a task to keep the file sorted. Any order, other than accession, demands that every new set of records has to be interpolated into the existing file series. Inordinately large files (say over 100,000 records) would require much time for sorting.

However, the debate concerning which type of file best suits a given situation is much more likely to hinge on the type of peripheral equipment available. Tape is cheap to use as a storage medium but limits the search procedure to sequential scanning. In computer terms the search time for a complete reel of tape is relatively slow, taking approximately ten minutes on a medium speed tape deck. If the required records are located at the middle of the tape, it can take the computer many minutes just to get at the wanted record. A common practice is to transfer the content of the tape onto disc for processing purposes, writing out onto tape at the end of the run. This gives in effect a direct access system. With this it is possible to call up any record by whatever key is being used, such as the accession number or the author. But note that files on disc give no saving whatever if the search requires every record to be vetted, for in that case a sequential progression through the file is going to be necessary whatever medium is used. The direct access system offers almost instant call up of any record in the file, no matter where it is physically located. This means that the strict sequencing of magnetic tape files is not necessary on random access devices.

Let us now examine one method of sorting complex files so that it is possible to produce catalogues in order of author, title, and so on. Assuming the availability of discs, a sort key is created for each type of record in the different files to be made. Thus the author and part of the title are extracted from each record, with an identifier such as the accession number by which it is then possible to call up the record on disc. From this run is created a file of authors with accession numbers, which is then sorted into alphabetical order. Since the file consists of records having only two elements, the size would keep the sorting time to a minimum. Once the file has been sorted, the accession number of each record in turn is used to call up the full record from the disc file. By this method one avoids the time consuming process of shuffling large amounts of data about to achieve a sorted file.

File order may not be particularly important until the need for a printout arises. From the point of view of processing it is the output requirements which dictate the need or otherwise for files in different orders. In an alphabetically ordered file one can reach the records relating to works by a given author by working through the alphabetical sequence until the correct name is found, whereas with direct access devices it is possible to reach such records directly *only* if authors are located at the front of each record as the key. If, as with a MARC structure, the author is hidden away in the record and access is only through the directory, it would still be necessary to vet every record in order to find all works by that one author. To sum up then, if most searches require that every record be vetted, there is almost no difference between storage devices in relation to speed and convenience. Where ordered files are used, then direct access devices offer considerable advantages in speed of access.

Other types of storage device may be used, such as magnetic cards or semi-photographic systems offering magnetic recordings of indexing data and photographic record of the textual matter. But whatever method is used the considerations which apply to magnetic tape and disc files would also apply to these other devices.

12
the data base as an index

CRITERIA

Once the data are input and processed, the system users are naturally interested in what type of question it is possible to put to the file. Theoretically it should be possible to put any type of question, but limitations do arise from both the way in which the programs have been constructed and the record format. The former governs the way in which file interrogation can be conducted, *ie* the number of parameters it is possible to cite, and the complexity of relationship which can be demanded. The question 'Have you a book by B C Vickery?' is a single parameter. On the other hand if one asks for the book by B C Vickery entitled *Techniques of information retrieval* published by Butterworth in 1970, we then have four parameters joined by the logical *and* device, for all four must be presented to effect a match. More complex relationships would obviously arise where subject terms were being used to formulate the question.

In the case of record format, we have already looked at the MARC structure and discovered that only by the provision of tags and subfield indicators in a variable field record is it possible to extract parts of the record without having to compare the question and record content character by character. The computer is quite capable of this, but in the case of very large files the time required would probably be unacceptable. The record may also carry a key; this, however, is not essential since the need for it depends on the way in which the file is interrogated at the first pass. If records are called up by author on the first pass, the placing of the author at the front (as the key) of each record allows this to be effected with maximum efficiency. It is also possible to have in place of, or in addition to, the key a string of bytes at the front of the record to give a binary coded

representation of the major contents in the file. Interrogation of this string is made to establish the relevance of a record. Where the interrogation of the file requires the scanning of each record until satisfactory recall is achieved, or until reaching a stipulated cut-off point (*eg* 50 items retrieved), the position of the records becomes irrelevant. This would arise when a number of parameters had to be matched using *or*, *eg* by given authors *or* emanating from given organisations. To meet such a situation every record has to be scanned. In this event either of the two possible file *orders* is satisfactory. The two orders are known as *sequential* and *random*.
Sequential order defines records which are arranged in a logical sequence, whether it be accession number, author, title, or subject. However, this order does not depend on the medium by which the records are stored, it being quite possible to achieve sequential order on magnetic tape, discs, drums or magnetic cards.
Random order indicates that records are placed on the file in whichever places are vacant. In the case of magnetic tape this would be following the last record entered on the file whereas on disc or drum it could be anywhere.

The real difference between these two arrangements is that:

Sequential order

a) requires each record to have a key by which it is ordered.

b) requires new records to be interpolated with those already on the file.

c) Assists the location of relevant parts of the file with the minimum of effort.

Random order

a) does not demand the use of keys.

b) does not require interpolation.

c) may require scanning the content of each record to determine matches.

It should be noted that this matter of order is not the same as *access*. This term covers the way in which we are able to get at the records once they have been filed, and procedure is dictated by the storage method used. As already shown, sequential and random order may be maintained on any device. When talking of access however, we recognise two methods irrespective of order: *serial* and *random*.

Serial means that it is possible to reach a given record only by examining every record preceding it in the sequence in which they occur. This obviously refers to magnetic tape and punched paper tape.
Random means that any record in the file may be called up directly, without the need to progress through from the start of the file. Such a term applies to discs, drums and magnetic cards.

What, then, is the possibility of searching for authors, titles, classes, etc, or even a combination of these? The answer is that searches of this kind will nearly always be possible, though some systems may offer less favourable conditions than others, in that the time taken to find relevant records may depend on the order in which the files are kept.

If we assume a *batch operating mode,* we will have to expect that a variety of searches will be fed simultaneously. Below are given four search situations:

1. Conferences on information processing, in English.
2. All works by B C Vickery.
3. Any item dealing with the use of laser recording techniques for the high density storage of textual data.
4. All introductory texts (for the layman) in science and technology, published during the last ten years.

These examples show the range which any large bibliographic file could be expected to meet, and a number of points arise from the searches as given. A file which was arranged in author order would suit searches such as number two very well. Looking at table below we see that no single file order will suit all the searches with equal

File	*Search*			
order	one	two	three	four
Author		x		
Title	?		?	?
Form	x		?	?
Date		?	?	?
Subject	x	?	x	?

x=match ?=possible match.

Relationship between the search and file order

facility, but that 'subject' would seem to offer the most generally helpful order. FIGURE 11.1 also shows that in some cases it may be possible to satisfy a search by mere intuition. A titles file could be searched for conferences having 'information processing' as part of the title, and this could yield a high proportion of those in the file. Similarly in search two, if B C Vickery had written almost exclusively in the field of information retrieval, a classified file might well produce most of the references to his works.

If one is trying to structure the file in a way which meets the maximum number of search situations, it is possible that the subject approach is to be preferred. However, as stated earlier, an ordered file requires continual interpolation of new records; a job which can be undesirably lengthy when associated with large volume files. However, compensation lies in the fact that the search times may be reduced, since any order file enables a large section of it to be rejected without examination or, at least, with the minimum of vetting.

We earlier assumed a batch mode operation, which entails the simultaneous presentation of various searches to the file. Because no order will satisfy every one of these, it may be necessary for the search to be conducted on each record individually. By this method the parameters are compared with the corresponding elements in the record and tested for a match. Where parameter requirements are satisfied, relevant details of the record are written out for inclusion in the final list. In this event the time spent ordering the file would seem to be without particular benefit. If the searches were always subject based however, the benefit can be realised since the subjects of all the searches would be sorted into the same order as the file and then matched against only the relevant parts of it.

In the case of on-line (real time) systems, interrogation of the file can be done at any time, since there is no need to batch the enquiries, and the person using the terminal can control the whole search process. The most significant advantage about using a terminal is that the success of a search can be adjudged as it progresses, thus enabling changes to be made as soon as unsatisfactory performance is detected. A greater amount of help can also be given to the enquirer to formulate his search. With off-line systems it is necessary to consult a printed dictionary or thesaurus of terms in order to translate the enquirer's needs into terms or class numbers used in the system. However, with the on-line search facility the enquirer could begin his interrogation by citing only one important term, and the terminal would then guide him to the most appropriate choice. Obviously a visual display unit would give the fastest response times, and it would therefore be usual practice for various alternative terms to be displayed in response to any one term fed in. Selecting one from the list shown would in turn cause the display of a further set of terms hierarchically lower or higher. As soon as the user was satisfied with the search profile, some sample matching records would be called up for display. These allow the user to assess the success of the search as the items displayed at that point can then be judged relevant or otherwise. In the event of the items not being particularly relevant, the user may either reform the search or, as a guide, request that the terms allotted to the items shown be displayed. This procedure helps to assess the cause for the search recovering unwanted items.

EXPRESSING CONCEPTS

Having said that subject order might well prove the most frequently required, and that on-line searches could be helped by the facility to broaden or narrow the specification, it would seem appropriate to look at the way in which concepts may be expressed. Our first and most obvious approach is through language, because this is the way we usually communicate. Could this be used to express the indexing characteristics of items on the file? We already use author's names, and though it is possible to reduce these to a code it would not be a convenient way of having to refer to them. However, in their natural form names present many difficulties as the *Anglo-American Cataloguing Rules* testify. It is therefore necessary to use just such rules to guarantee uniformity between the way in which an author is entered on the file and the way in which that author is cited in the search profile. An alternative would be to have the computer generate from the author name an index of alternative forms which would be scanned before a search was begun.

In the case of subject concepts, it has been common practice to use words in catalogues, indexes and mechanised information retrieval systems. In recent years there has been considerable incentive to examine the need for control over any language used for machine indexing. Such services as *Chemical titles*, and the index to *Biological abstracts* called *BASIC* (Biological Abstracts Subject in Context) use the words as they appear in the titles of the articles being indexed. This means there is no attempt to standardise the different forms of terms, or to establish connections between related terms. The protagonist for these type of KWIC (keyword-in-context) indexes make the valid point that the pressure of present literature output requires that indexing be wholly mechanised. Certainly the speed at which such indexes can be produced underlines their convenience. However, it is also possible to use natural language generating the indexing from an abstract of the document or from the complete text rather than just the titles. This can all be done automatically by the computer. However, these methods of semantic analysis are not yet sufficiently tried and tested to establish any real confidence in their results (Artandi, 1968).

The use of a controlled language is not new. Compilers of dictionary catalogues have always had to maintain an authority file often based on a published list of subject headings, *eg* Sears. With the growth in the use of post-coordinate retrieval systems, many lists or thesauri have been produced containing the terms likely to occur in an index relating to a certain subject area. An exceptional example, illustrating as it does the importance of a systematic approach to thesaurus construction, is that of the English Electric Company (1970). The use of such lists enable concepts to be chosen appropriately and consistently at indexing or search stage. For those who have not met up with the term 'post-coordinate' it will suffice to say that such a system allows the searcher to express his needs by combining or coordinating any concepts expressed in the system. The alternative is the pre-coordinate system which presents the searcher with fixed combinations which may or may not accord with his needs as expressed.

Most readers will be aware of the possibility of expressing subjects notationally, using letters or numbers, or both, instead of words. Many classification schemes are available offering both pre- and post-coordinate systems. The Dewey Decimal Classification is the most widely used example of the former, while the Universal Decimal Classification and Colon Classification offer, in differing degrees, the facility for post-coordination. The use of a notation provides a further aid to the searcher, so that the subjects covered by the scheme may be divided hierarchically, which could be reflected in the notational structure. Thus in the Dewey scheme we have:

800 Literature
820 English literature
822 English drama
822.3 Elizabethan period
822.33 William Shakespeare

By reading the notation from right to left one is able to deduce that each digit relates to a subset of the class indicated by all the preceding digits. This has implications for any search procedure since the failure of a class number to recall wanted items can be offset by broadening the search to the preceding hierarchical level. This can be effected by dropping the righthand digit in the example above. For a computer based system however, this notation would have to be applied consistently throughout, or otherwise offer predictable areas of exception.

In the case of synthetic classification schemes (in contrast to an enumerative scheme such as Dewey) class numbers may be built up at the time of indexing, so that there is a possibility of displaying within the notation the facets of a complex subject. Thus the subject of *Architectural plans for marble museums in Great Britain in the twentieth century* could be written out as the following string: architectural; museums; marble; plans; Great Britain; twentieth century, and might be expressed in the notation of the Colon Classification as:

NA, 6 ; 3 : 3 . 561 'N

The particular point to note here is that each facet, introduced as it is by a unique symbol or indicator, could be recognised by a machine search. Therefore, Colon permits the identification of parts of a class number from an examination of the separate facet indicators wherever located, by the class marks to which they relate. The UDC also offers such a facility with the various signs for form, place, etc.

Whilst it can be seen that conventional class numbers are perfectly suitable for machine searching, less clear is the ability of such numbers to provide a satisfactory analysis of the subject content of items to be indexed. In cases where enumerative schemes like Dewey are concerned, it is often assumed that the classifier has to content himself with a summary of the subject content by using the most appropriate number. However, there is no reason why more than one number should not be used so that every significant topic in the title is recorded in the system. This matter of exhaustivity (the degree to which concepts within a document are represented in the index) applies equally to systems which use natural language terms instead of a notation. Consideration has to be given not only to the number of concepts recognised in the system, but also to the level or degree of specificity with which the index language shall express concepts. Many enumerative classification schemes are unable to record the detailed sub-divisions at every level and therefore a containing class may have to be used. By using natural language there is really no limitation on the number of words which can be used and therefore any level of concept can be expressed. This is not to say that such languages will automatically provide such a facility, since, particularly in areas of fringe relationship to the main subject of the index, it may be considered unnecessary to provide highly specific terms.

FILE ORDER

Having allotted terms or class numbers to each item, we are still faced with the decision about the way in which we will arrange the file. Firstly there is the possibility that the file is extremely large and that any requirement to repeat records would be unacceptable. In such cases there can be but one record per item and the indexing data will have to be located within it. Apart from the random order, it is quite feasible to treat such a file in a similar manner to books located on shelves. Thus we would have a one place scheme which, though not ideal, is certainly quite practicable. Just as with books, items would have to be interpolated into the sequence. Since, though, such operations would always involve writing out to new storage areas there is no equivalent to moving all the books around to make room for a new intake.

Where exhaustive or *depth indexing* is used every record in turn will either have to be scanned for possible matching with a search requirement, or a special search file will be provided. Such a search file would offer as many entry points as would be compatible with, though not necessarily equal to, the concepts indexed for each item. At each entry point would be a term or class number together with item details abbreviated as much as possible. In the case of class numbers we have a numeric sequence with some item details ranged under each number. With subject terms or *descriptors* we have an alphabetic sequence of item data. This file arrangement is known as *inverted* order since the indexing data for each item is distributed throughout the file. If we think in terms of direct access devices, the inverted file need only have a unique number by which to identify the items ranged under each term. Such numbers can be used to call up the full detail of the item from a master file. Call up could be carried out as a normal part of the search routine, so that the subject search is made first and further parameters sought in records selected by the first screening.

SEARCH METHOD

It is not the intention of this book to discuss in detail the various ways in which a search request may be presented, but in general there are three methods of presentation: *a*) Complete match, *b*) Boolean statement and *c*) Weighted term search. Using the first method, all terms in the search have to be associated with the item for it to be relevant. Using the second certain permutations of terms in the search will be required for relevancy to be determined, while with the last, terms are given a numeric weight in accordance with their importance to the user, which gives a result ranked according to score. Thus items with the highest score are listed or displayed first.

However, the subject approach could be only one of the wanted parameter sets, and it may therefore be necessary to include others, such as author, language, date, and format. If the file is arranged by subject, a search is first made for items in the required class. Once located, the parameter next listed in the search is sought in the record. If this has to be present for a match, its absence would indicate that the record was being rejected without further scanning. If this is not mandatory, its presence or absence is noted and the next parameter is then sought. Thus once the search procedure has selected appropriate subject sections (classes) of the file, each record in them is then examined for matching against the other parameters in the search profile.

With fixed field format, it would be possible to reach the relevant parts of each record by stating in the search which parts (indicated by the character positions) are to be examined for a match. In the case of the variable field format, however, the character positions are not known, and it is therefore necessary to state the type of elements to be examined in each record and leave the computer to find them. Taking the MARC record as typical of a variable field record (FIGURE 25), you will see that the only way in which the computer can find an element is by reference to the directory. Having an instruction to locate a given element with the tag number 100 (personal author), the directory is searched, twelve characters at a time (this is the set relating to any one field) to discover if there is a field of that number and where it is located in the record. Since the entries in the directory are arranged in numerical order of tags, as are the fields themselves, the first tag in the search is compared with the first in the directory. If the tag in the search profile is higher, it is then compared with the next entry in the directory. This process is continued until there is a match or the search tag is shown to be lower, in which case the sought tag must be absent.

Once the required field is discovered, the computer seeks out the content and makes this available for comparison with the data given in the search profile. In this case then, the author given in field 100 is compared with the requested author. If there is no match, and the author was given as a mandatory parameter, the record is rejected without further examination. If the author was optional, the next tag given in the search profile is sought, and so on until all the tags have been exhausted. Therefore in the case of a classified file, this procedure is carried out on every record having a relevant class number.

As a last point in this chapter, it must be said that that which has been outlined above has assumed that initially the subject of the search is a mandatory part of the profile. Were this not so, any savings offered by a file in classified sequence vanish. When a search requires the permutation of various parameters without having one type in common, no order is any better than another, and therefore every record in turn must be searched. However, even in this case there is one saving possible. Those permutations in the search which contain parameters used to order the file can be put directly to the relevant parts, while those with other parameters have to be put to each record regardless of their place in the file.

13
output by mechanical line printers

It is perhaps in the area of computer output that there is the most controversy amongst librarians. As was explained in the chapters covering peripherals, the line printer usually provided for outputting data from the computer, can work at anything from 1,000 to 1,500 lines a minute allowing up to 160 characters a line. But these speeds require a limited character set to keep the barrel carrying the type to the minimum possible circumference. Thus one finds that all high speed barrel printers have upper case only. This together with the need to print everything simultaneously on one line, undoubtedly deters many users who expect the quality of output which they are accustomed to receiving from conventional printers.

First we should distinguish between what may be called 'work prints' and those intended for library use, which we shall call 'user prints'. Under the term work prints would be classed such lists as those of items on loan, book selection lists and books on order. User prints include the catalogue, bibliographies, selective lists provided to individuals or groups on a regular basis (known as SDI—selective dissemination of information), and the like. Quite obviously the work prints have a relatively short life and are intended for the use of staff who can become acclimatised to their rather utilitarian appearance. Since these lists will require frequent updating and therefore reprinting, speed of output has a definite merit. In the case of user prints certain qualities of legibility and attractiveness are desirable.

Although the speed at which a line printer is run sounds considerable, it is nevertheless unable to keep pace with the operating speeds of the computer. It is therefore usual to buffer the data to be printed so that the processing run does not have to be restricted to the speed of the printer. All the data for printing must be formatted in the correct sequence for output. This of course is part of the program routine, but also required is a print program which arranges the data on paper. Take the sample entry in FIGURE 27. As can be seen the record has been printed out in its entirety without any attempt at arranging the data in an order other than that in store. In effect the data have been printed out as they occur in the record up to a maximum of (in this case) eighty characters per line, and as many lines as necessary. The next record would be printed in the same way with, for example, five blank lines between each record.

This apparently simple output still requires a library program which may be available as a standard sub-routine automatically available from the suite of programs held in store. Such output would not be acceptable for any but the most utilitarian purpose. The program operates by taking each line full of characters from the record and passing them to the printer. It will be noticed that there is no regard for the point at which the line breaks the text. It is quite common to find words arbitrarily broken. The cases where such unsightly output may be justified is when its life will be short and its use administrative as in selection lists and check lists. Note, however, that even these can be formatted to assist scanning and that the only practical reason for obtaining a full printout of the record is when the total content of the record is to be checked. Thus selection of works themselves, and at the same time a scan through the record content for data (like class number) not compatible with local practice may use such printouts. Similarly the complete record content would be required when a check is being made for failures or errors occurring during processing runs. Certainly such output is not particularly helpful to those searching for a small number of elements in each record, since it is not obvious just where such an element will appear in the printed version. It is therefore more satisfactory to have programs which produce printed copy suited to the intended use.

Despite the fact that upper case only is used, the layout will afford considerable help in locating relevant information from a page full of entries. Such copy might comprise: selection lists, accessions lists, on-orders lists, loans lists (including overdues and reserves), statistics, notifications and orders, catalogues and bibliographies (user prints) and diagnostics. Each of these would require a certain layout. Thus the selection list may have class number on the first line, author and title on the next and subsequent lines, and imprint on a following line. On-order lists might well be in author order and would therefore have the author on the first line of entry, the rest being on subsequent lines, while the supplier and date of order may be set out to one side for ease of checking. On the other hand the loans list will be in columns, one in order of borrower the other in order of item borrowed.

Obviously the catalogue may be set out in any way desired, and although many libraries restrict each entry to one or two lines, it should be noted that this is not obligatory. In the case of catalogues certain restrictions are presented by the large amounts to be printed and by the need to enable users to scan entries quickly. It is for this reason that the two line entry is favoured, allowing as it does the display of some twenty to forty entries per page, as can be seen in FIGURE 28. Another approach is to display the entries in two columns, each entry having the layout of the conventional catalogue card. This is of course more wasteful but is rather easier to read (FIGURE 29).

It is possible to use the printer to generate orders to suppliers and recall notices to borrowers. All the relevant data are made available to the print program which in turn pays out the entry on pre-printed forms. Note that the full width of the printer may be used by the expedient of arranging the forms alongside each other, thus printing more than one entry at a time. Once printed, the stationery is separated to give single sets for each entry. While on the topic of orders, it is worth pointing out that most printers will produce up to six copies (a top copy and five carbons). In practice it will be found that with heavy papers three carbon copies are the most which can be produced in readable condition. It is also possible to produce any width of stationery within the limits of the printer, so that, allowing for margins, it is feasible to have forms four or eighteen inches wide, giving a line length of forty or 160 characters.

The *diagnostic* is always necessary, as it is the means by which the system operators can check that everything is working correctly during the runs. It is common practice to require the production of a diagnostic printout during processing, so that if the run does produce errors, the reason for their occurrence may be traced. It can also be seen as a checking device for the data before or after being processed. Obviously such a printout needs to be presented to afford maximum assistance in detecting the cause of errors. Therefore every computer has a standard set of codes which are used in diagnostics to indicate the reason either for standard errors occurring or for the rejection of the data submitted.

Since it is possible to arrange the output in any way desired, there is no reason against producing all statistics on the high speed printer. The print program can provide headings for the columns and display the figures accurately aligned. Statistics covering expenditure, loans, readership and the like, will originally come from the regular process runs. However, there is no need to collate and analyse these every time, as the figures can be cumulated and processed for a statistical printout at monthly intervals or less frequently.

Despite the seemingly high speed at which line printers can operate, there is every need to ensure that the demands for output are kept realistic. The total amount of printing required should be related to the time needed to produce a single page of fanfold. It should be remembered that it is the rate at which the paper is fed through the printer which will govern the speed, so that no time will be saved if a line is blank though it is possible to skip a series of lines. If the fanfold page has sixty lines, no more than fifty four would be used, thereby allowing some space at the top and bottom of the page. If the printer works at 1,200 lines a minute and each entry is printed out on two lines, the twenty pages printed in one minute will contain 540 entries. If the list or catalogue has 54,000 items the print time will be more than 100 minutes. However it is desirable to have a gap at intervals to assist reading or merely to emphasise a natural break in the sequence (a change of letter or class). In this event one might waste a further six lines per page. Such a seemingly small change to layout would increase the output time by ten minutes and result in the use of 200 more pages of continuous stationery. Thus it is essential not to be over optimistic in one's expectations of the line printer's output capabilities.

Whilst the barrel printer is operated at high speed it can, as stated previously, produce only upper case output from a rather limited character set. Should you wish for lower case and possibly an extended character set, the chain printer can be used. However, because of the way in which this works, the printing speeds may be down to as low as 100 lines a minute according to the number of characters in the set. Such a reduction is no small matter when high volume output is required. To regain the speed and still permit the use of an extensive range of non-standard characters takes us into the realms of photocomposition and the like, which will be discussed in the next chapter.

One vexing problem has also to be faced in connection with the use of printers. It was pointed out earlier that only four usable copies can be produced at one pass. In cases where multiple copies are needed use can be made of the various duplicating methods available. One point must be made here, and that is the rather indifferent quality of computer continuous paper. Many computer installations are at pains to buy paper at a competitive price. This leads to bulk ordering of one type only, which in turn may mean all output without special stationery is issued on lined paper. Such lines aid the eye across a sixteen inch page, but can also interfere with the readability of the text. The paper is often rather thin which makes handling difficult when collated into book form.

As inspection of any computer paper will reveal, it is necessary to have sprocket holes on each side at half inch intervals to ensure the paper passes through the printer without slipping. Once printed, the paper can be guillotined in various ways. It is quite possible to cut off the perforated edges, and make cuts down the page, as well as across. The same machine will also stack as it cuts. Note that this is not the same as collating, since if the pages are split down the middle there would be two stacks produced which would have to be merged manually. But at least as each page is cut the resultant two would be placed on top of the two before.

If computer paper is to be kept between covers having twin or triple post anchors, it can be useful to leave the perforations on the lefthand side. Sometimes, though, the paper is scored just inside the perforations to assist their removal, in which case one may find that pages begin to come adrift if they are in service for too long a period.

14
other forms of output

Although multiple copies of user prints can be made by repetitive runs using the mechanical printer, this method may not be possible in the light of other user demands. It is therefore useful to be aware of alternative ways of producing numerous copies. Various systems have been developed which convert digital information displaying the result as graphics or text. This is achieved by the program generation of images or by the use of matrices carrying alpha-numerics and displaying either onto a cathode ray tube (visual display unit), or direct onto a recording surface. These machines can be on-line or off-line using magnetic tape, punched tape or card, and in some cases keyboard input.

NON-MECHANICAL LINE PRINTERS

The first group of printers in this section may be thought of as equivalent to the mechanical line printer in that (with some exceptions) they have a limited character set and perform similar functions. On some machines it is possible to print out direct onto continuous paper electrostatically, which would give only one copy at a time. A point to remember here is that the text can be optically reduced so that a given output could be fitted onto less paper than with a mechanical printer.

These machines can also produce microforms which include roll film (16mm or 35mm), microfiche at various reductions or aperture cards. Texts and graphics displayed on a cathode ray tube face are recorded on film, which in turn can be used to produce further copies. One has the option of same size duplication, further reduction or hardcopy.

Microforms certainly offer considerable savings, but their use assumes the availability of good quality readers in sufficient quantity.

In this connection one should remember that fiche is cheap to reproduce but not particularly easy to use. Loading fiche correctly requires some dexterity, while searching for a frame containing the required entry can be tedious. By contrast, roll film in cassettes used with the machines having automatic take up (so that the film does not have to be manually threaded) are virtually foolproof. Such machines also afford high speed traverse and can incorporate search aids such as footage counters or index marks which indicate the position of each frame relative to the end of the reel.

Having produced a microfilm copy from magnetic tape, a further refinement is now possible with the use of ultrafiche, especially PCMI (photochromic microimage) developed by NCR. This is now being used by the British National Bibliography for the cumulative output of the newly entitled *Books in English*. Over three thousand images can be recorded on a fiche six inches by four. This means that a catalogue containing some hundred thousand entries can be updated by the computer and the result output on two fiche, assuming that one image could contain twenty or more entries.

The success of microform provision must rest on the adequacy of machines provided for viewing. These need to be simple to operate, efficient in varying light conditions and durable. Assistance in the evaluation of viewers and comparative assessment is provided in this country by the National Reprographic Centre for Documentation (*see* references).

If the microform itself is not considered suitable as a user print substitute, the 16 or 35mm film generated by the computer can be used to produce hardcopy or even offset masters. This might seem to invalidate any savings made from using the computer, but at least the updating, which would normally involve interfiling, is done automatically. This is a task which the computer manages admirably and which, without tedious human effort, enables the continual production of revised catalogues, indexes and the like.

FILMSETTERS

The use of filmsetters gives the equivalent of conventionally printed text and can incorporate illustrative matter. One example of such equipment is the Photon Lumizip 900, known widely as GRACE (graphic arts composing equipment) which is in use at the National

Library of Medicine for the production of *Index medicus*. Such machines can operate at speeds varying between 300 and six thousand characters per second according to design. Control is effected by off-line punched paper tape or magnetic tape, or on-line. Two basic methods are employed to achieve the extensive character set and sizes. The first has a matrix containing one or more founts positioned behind lenses which control size, so that light passing through the matrix at the appropriate place then passes through an optical system and is projected direct onto film. The second method generates the characters by program and displays the result on a cathode ray tube, which is then photographed. Those who would like to know more about the design and capabilities of filmsetters could not do better than consult the excellently detailed survey provided by Arthur H Phillips in 1968 (*see* bibliography).

TERMINALS

It will no doubt be some years before libraries use terminals to any significant extent but nevertheless it is worthwhile considering the effect their use has on output format. One point of particular importance is the type of terminal involved. If use is made of teletypewriters, the speeds of display will be lower than with cathode ray tube units. However the former produces hardcopy, which is a great advantage if large numbers of references are required.

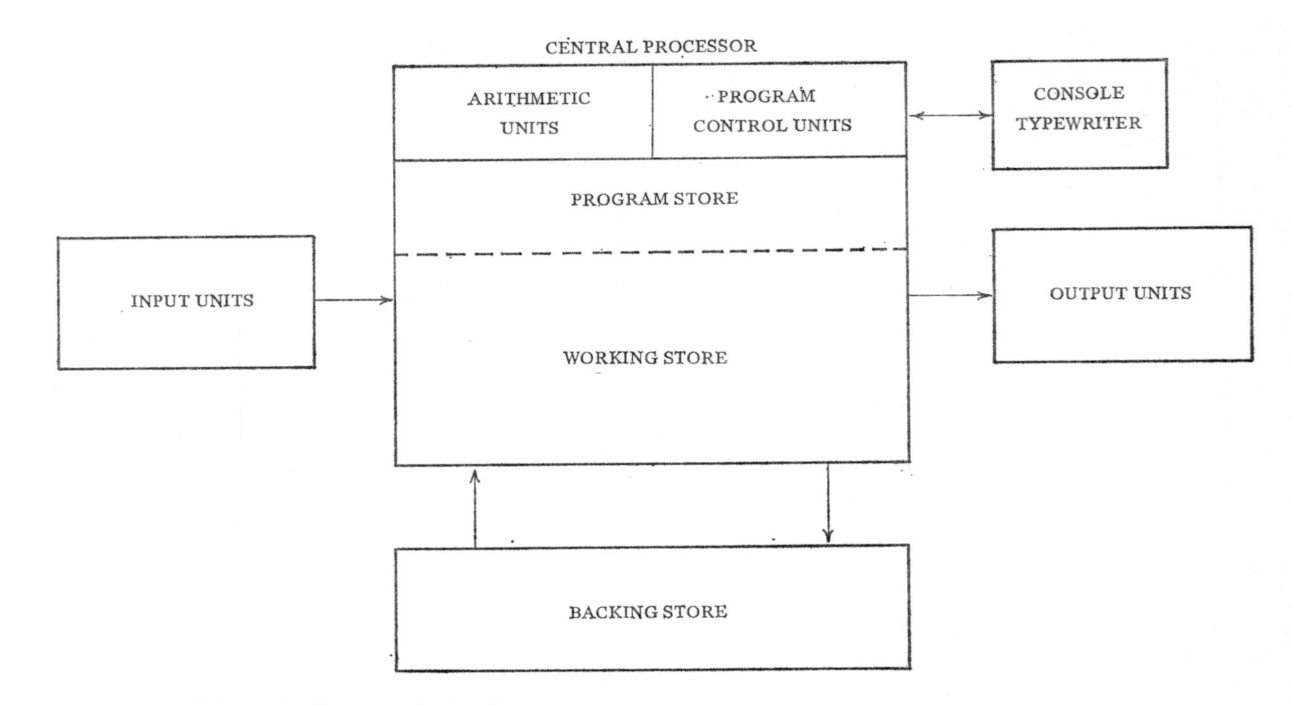

FIGURE 1 Schematic diagram of a batch processor.

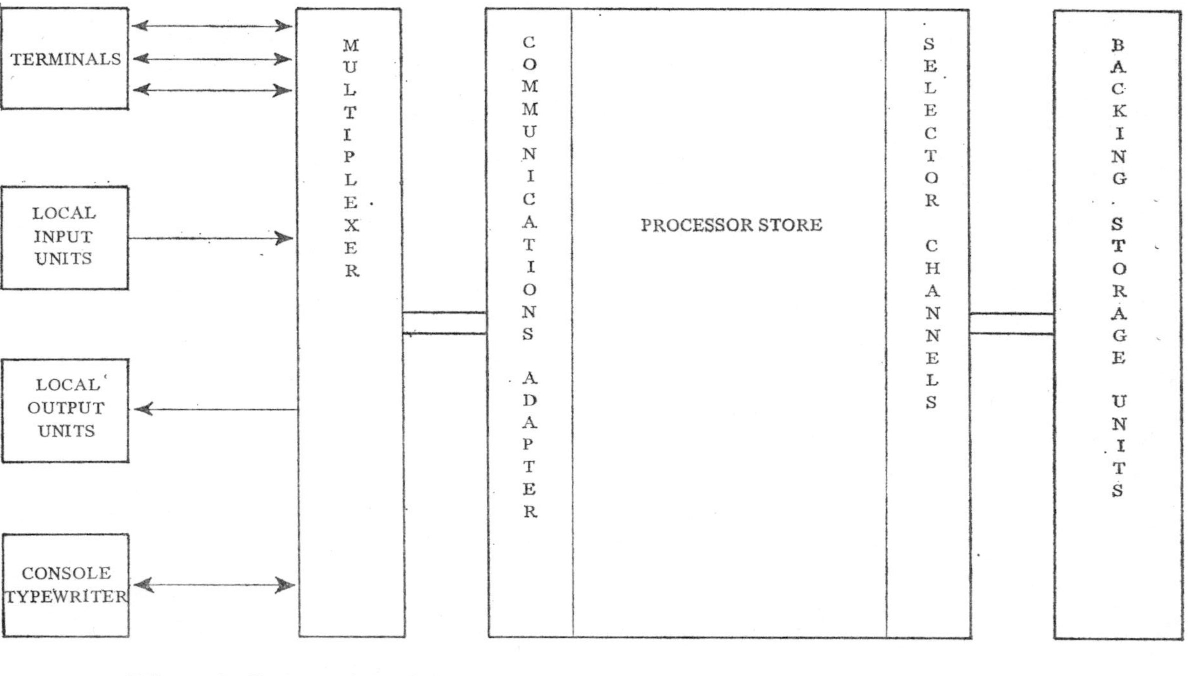

FIGURE 2 Schematic diagram of a real-time processor.

A B C D E F G H I J K L M N O P Q R S T U V W X Y Z & 0 1 2 3 4 5 6 7 8 9

0 0 0 0 0 0 0 0 0 0 0 0 0 0 0 0 0 0 0 0 0 0 0 0 0 0 0 0 0 0 0 0 0 0 0 0 0 0 0 0 0 0 0 0 0 0 0 0 0 0 0 0 0 0 0 0 0 0 0 0 0 0 0 0 0 0 0 0 0 0 0 0 0 0 0 0 0 0 0 0

1 2 3 4 5 6 7 8 9 10 11 12 13 14 15 16 17 18 19 20 21 22 23 24 25 26 27 28 29 30 31 32 33 34 35 36 37 38 39 40 41 42 43 44 45 46 47 48 49 50 51 52 53 54 55 56 57 58 59 60 61 62 63 64 65 66 67 68 69 70 71 72 73 74 75 76 77 78 79 80

1 1 1 1 1 1 1 1 1 1 1 1 1 1 1 1 1 1 1 1 1 1 1 1 1 1 1 1 1 1 1 1 1 1 1 1 1 1 1 1 1 1 1 1 1 1 1 1 1 1 1 1 1 1 1 1 1 1 1 1 1 1 1 1 1 1 1 1 1 1 1 1 1 1 1 1 1 1 1 1

2 2 2 2 2 2 2 2 2 2 2 2 2 2 2 2 2 2 2 2 2 2 2 2 2 2 2 2 2 2 2 2 2 2 2 2 2 2 2 2 2 2 2 2 2 2 2 2 2 2 2 2 2 2 2 2 2 2 2 2 2 2 2 2 2 2 2 2 2 2 2 2 2 2 2 2 2 2 2 2

3 3 3 3 3 3 3 3 3 3 3 3 3 3 3 3 3 3 3 3 3 3 3 3 3 3 3 3 3 3 3 3 3 3 3 3 3 3 3 3 3 3 3 3 3 3 3 3 3 3 3 3 3 3 3 3 3 3 3 3 3 3 3 3 3 3 3 3 3 3 3 3 3 3 3 3 3 3 3 3

4 4 4 4 4 4 4 4 4 4 4 4 4 4 4 4 4 4 4 4 4 4 4 4 4 4 4 4 4 4 4 4 4 4 4 4 4 4 4 4 4 4 4 4 4 4 4 4 4 4 4 4 4 4 4 4 4 4 4 4 4 4 4 4 4 4 4 4 4 4 4 4 4 4 4 4 4 4 4 4

5 5 5 5 5 5 5 5 5 5 5 5 5 5 5 5 5 5 5 5 5 5 5 5 5 5 5 5 5 5 5 5 5 5 5 5 5 5 5 5 5 5 5 5 5 5 5 5 5 5 5 5 5 5 5 5 5 5 5 5 5 5 5 5 5 5 5 5 5 5 5 5 5 5 5 5 5 5 5 5

6 6 6 6 6 6 6 6 6 6 6 6 6 6 6 6 6 6 6 6 6 6 6 6 6 6 6 6 6 6 6 6 6 6 6 6 6 6 6 6 6 6 6 6 6 6 6 6 6 6 6 6 6 6 6 6 6 6 6 6 6 6 6 6 6 6 6 6 6 6 6 6 6 6 6 6 6 6 6 6

7 7 7 7 7 7 7 7 7 7 7 7 7 7 7 7 7 7 7 7 7 7 7 7 7 7 7 7 7 7 7 7 7 7 7 7 7 7 7 7 7 7 7 7 7 7 7 7 7 7 7 7 7 7 7 7 7 7 7 7 7 7 7 7 7 7 7 7 7 7 7 7 7 7 7 7 7 7 7 7

8 8 8 8 8 8 8 8 8 8 8 8 8 8 8 8 8 8 8 8 8 8 8 8 8 8 8 8 8 8 8 8 8 8 8 8 8 8 8 8 8 8 8 8 8 8 8 8 8 8 8 8 8 8 8 8 8 8 8 8 8 8 8 8 8 8 8 8 8 8 8 8 8 8 8 8 8 8 8 8

9 9 9 9 9 9 9 9 9 9 9 9 9 9 9 9 9 9 9 9 9 9 9 9 9 9 9 9 9 9 9 9 9 9 9 9 9 9 9 9 9 9 9 9 9 9 9 9 9 9 9 9 9 9 9 9 9 9 9 9 9 9 9 9 9 9 9 9 9 9 9 9 9 9 9 9 9 9 9 9

1 2 3 4 5 6 7 8 9 10 11 12 13 14 15 16 17 18 19 20 21 22 23 24 25 26 27 28 29 30 31 32 33 34 35 36 37 38 39 40 41 42 43 44 45 46 47 48 49 50 51 52 53 54 55 56 57 58 59 60 61 62 63 64 65 66 67 68 69 70 71 72 73 74 75 76 77 78 79 80

Dataset Limited A member of the ICL group of companies 00-354 Printed in the U.K.

FIGURE 3 80 column card punching code.

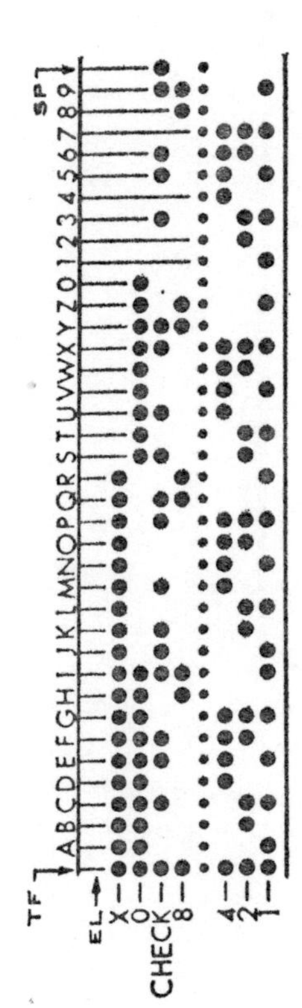

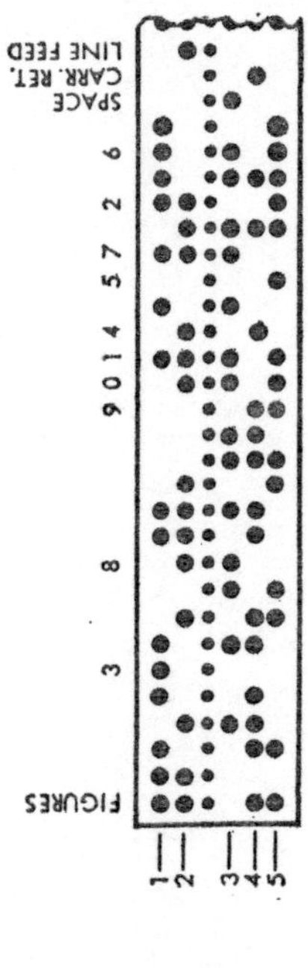

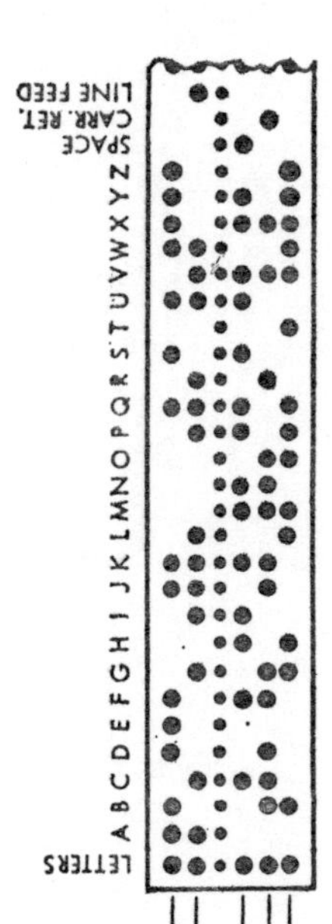

FIGURE 4 Examples of five and eight track codes.

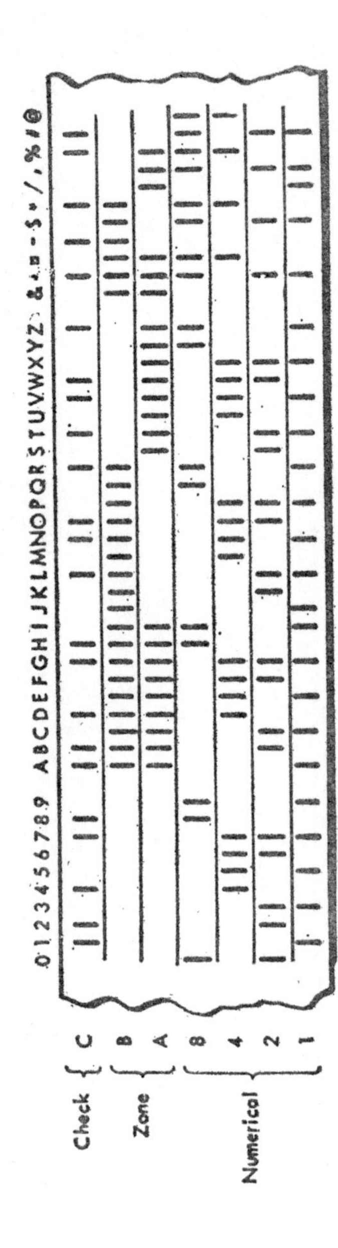

FIGURE 5 Representative computer magnetic tape coding.

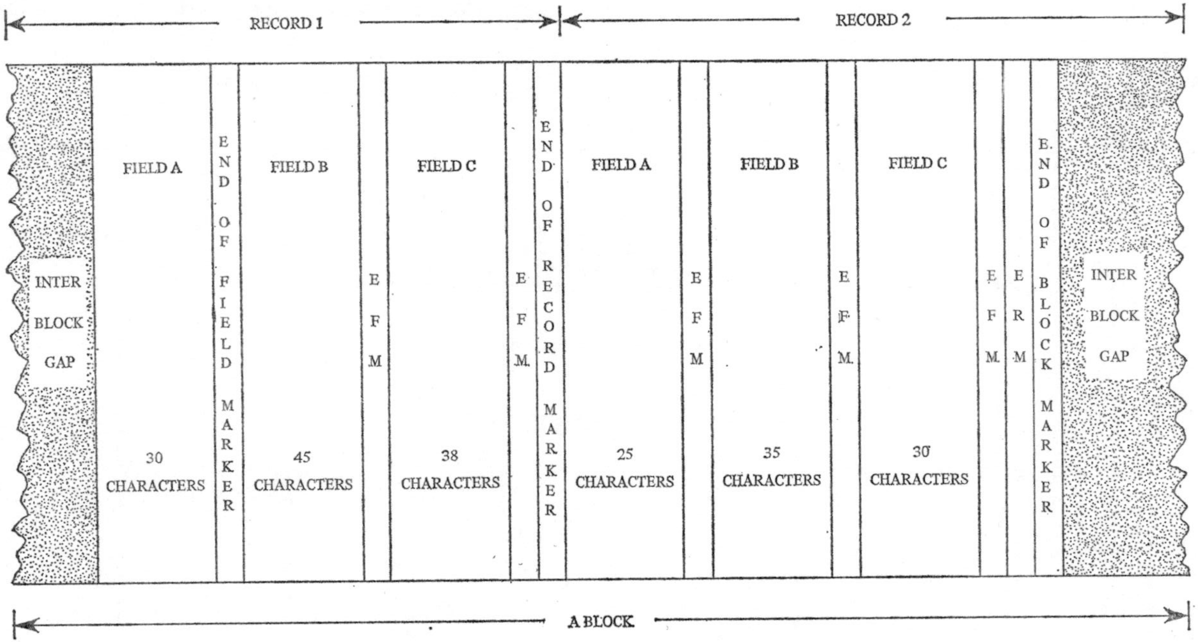

RECORD 1

RECORD 2

INTER BLOCK GAP

FIELD A 30 CHARACTERS

END OF FIELD MARKER

FIELD B 45 CHARACTERS

EFM

FIELD C 38 CHARACTERS

EFM

END OF RECORD MARKER

FIELD A 25 CHARACTERS

EFM

FIELD B 35 CHARACTERS

EFM

FIELD C 30 CHARACTERS

EFM

ERM

END OF BLOCK MARKER

INTER BLOCK GAP

A BLOCK

FIGURE 6 Example of layout of variable length data on magnetic tape.

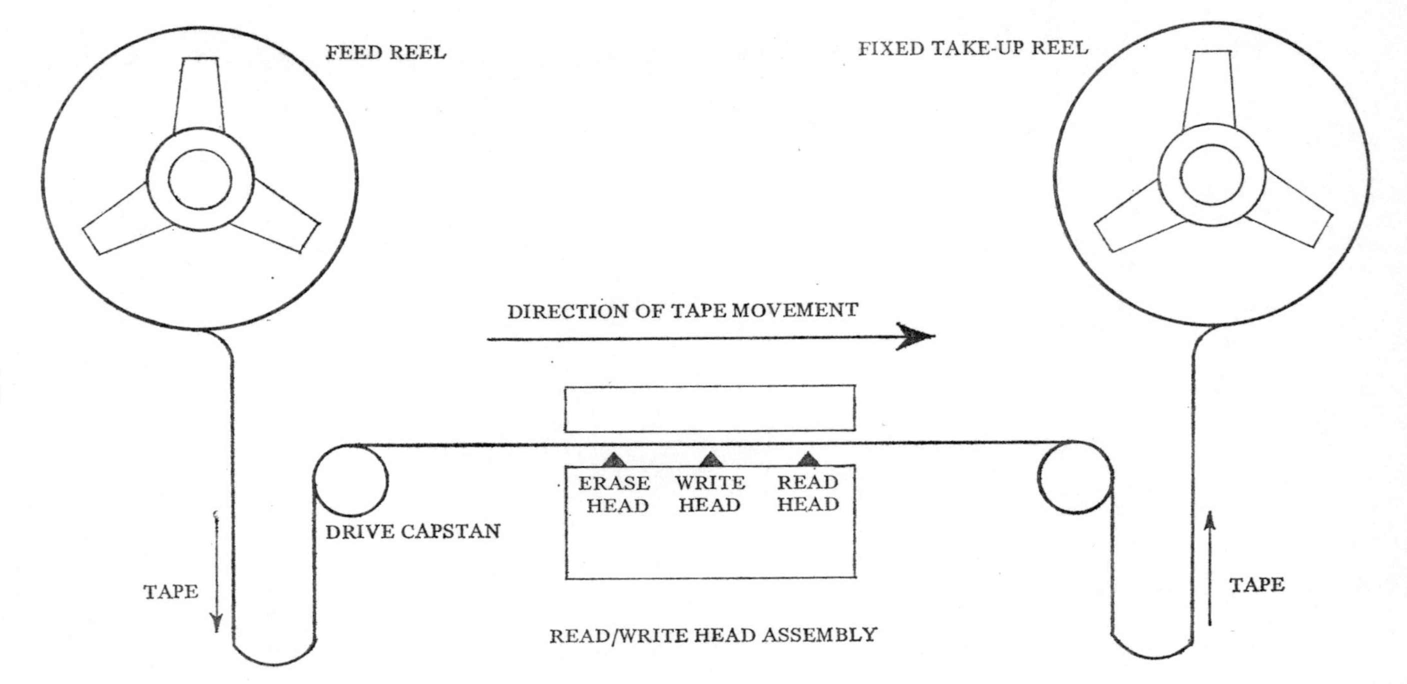

FIGURE 7 Schematic diagram of magnetic tape deck.

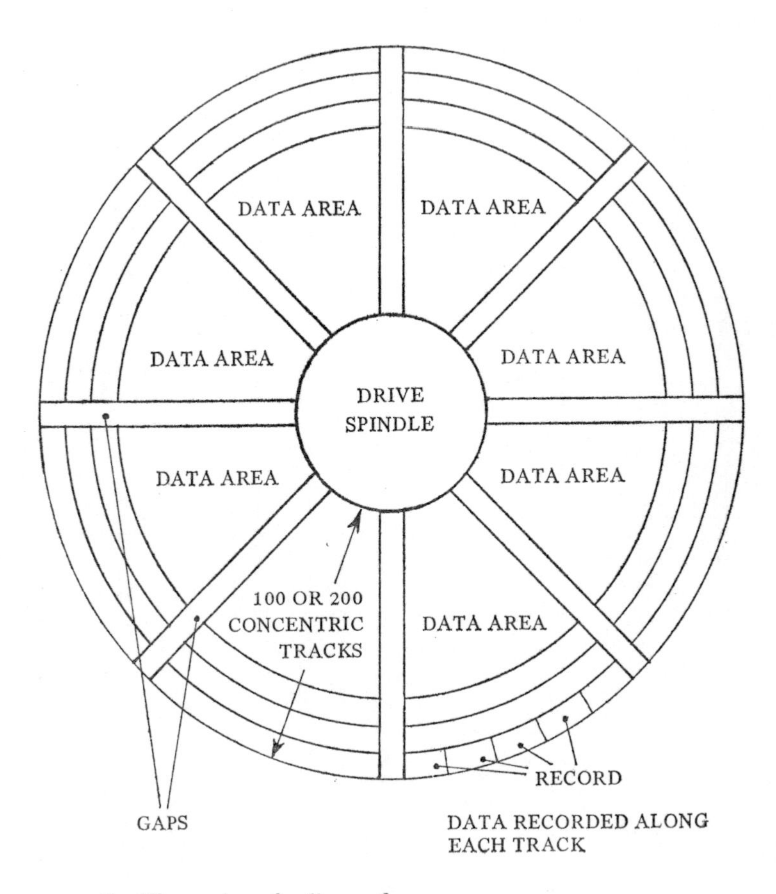

FIGURE 8 Illustration of a disc surface.

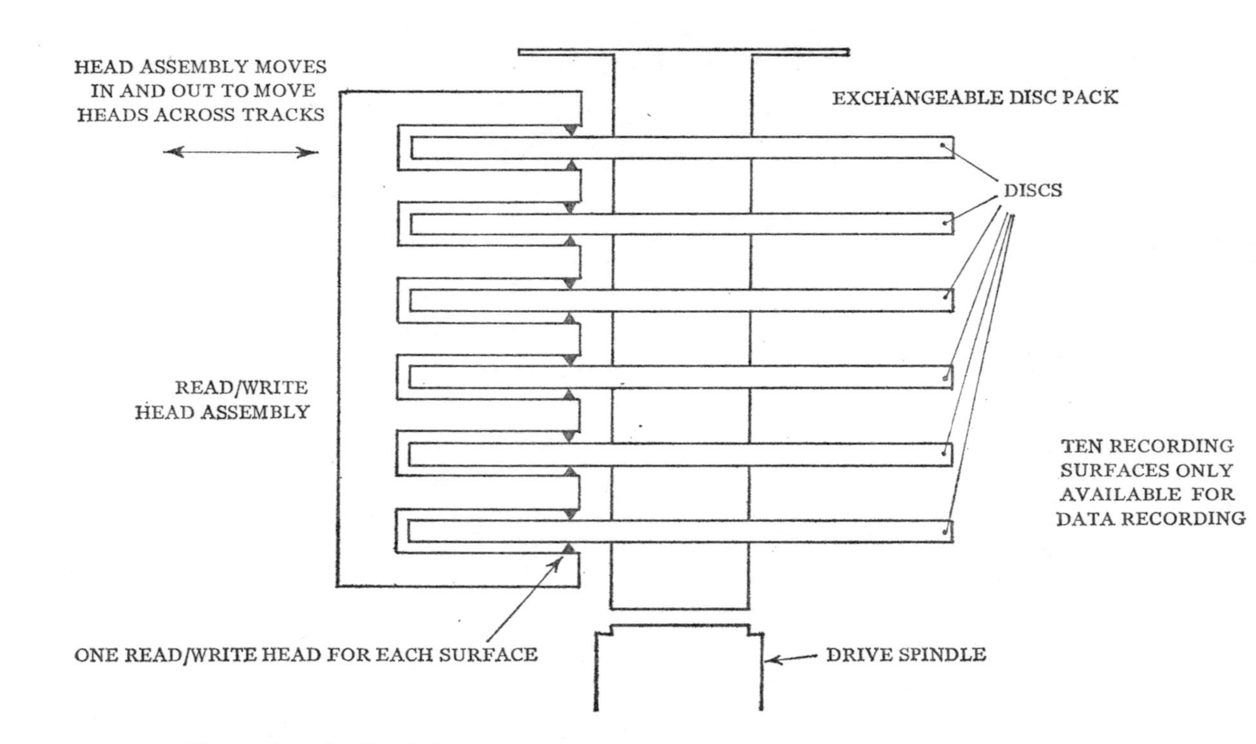

FIGURE 9 Illustration of a disc drive.

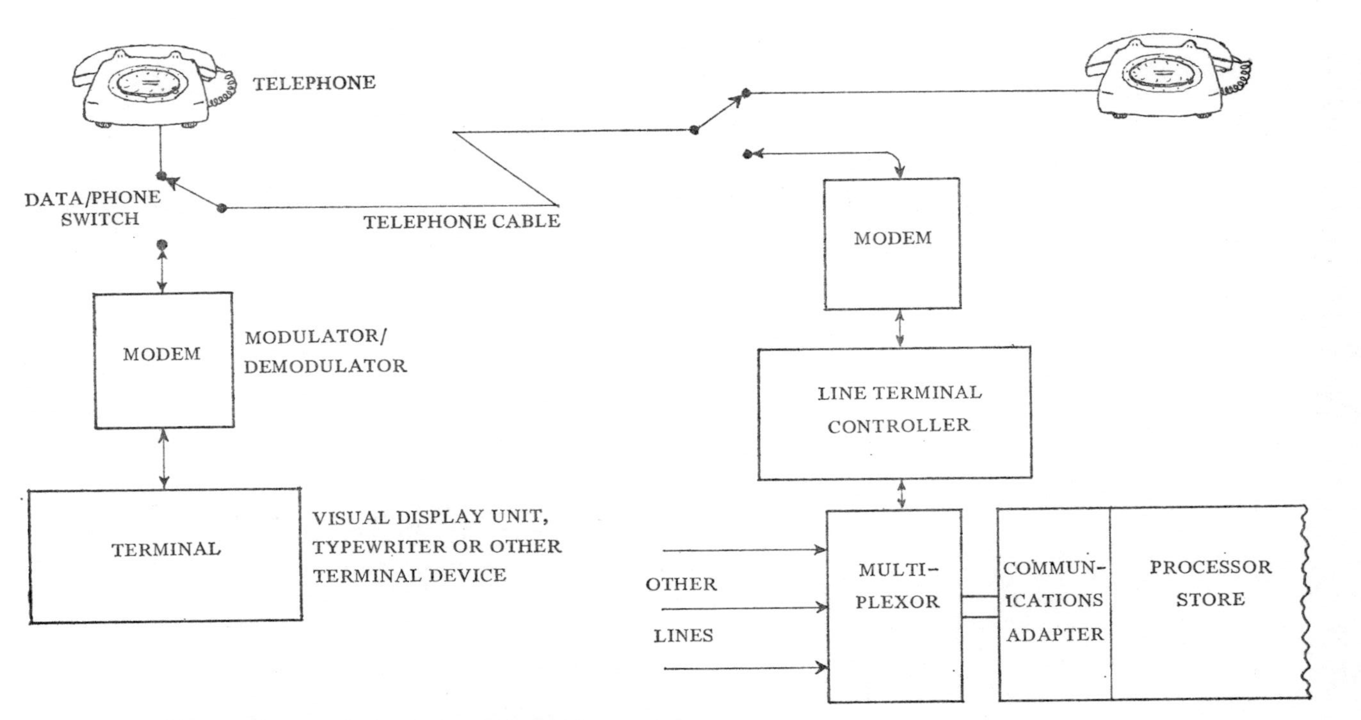

FIGURE 10 Terminal transmission link using telephone cable.

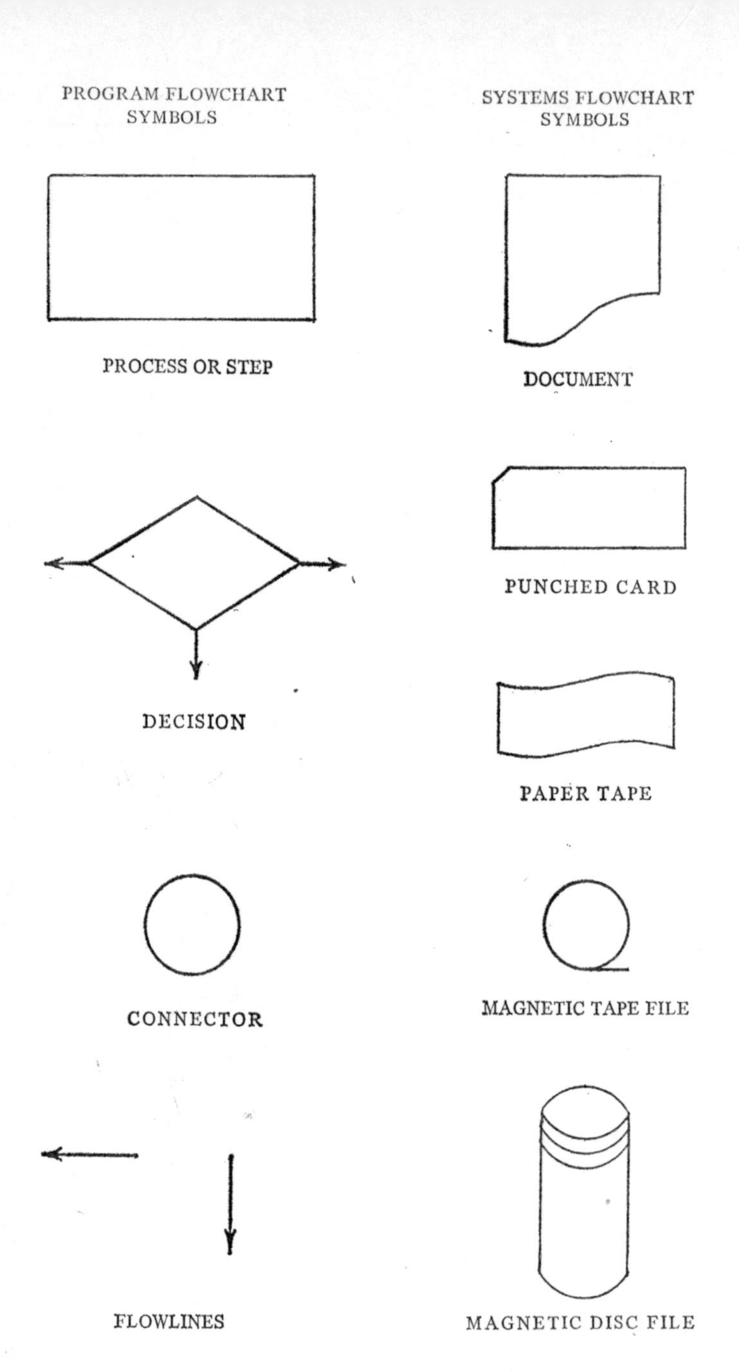

FIGURE 11 A selection of program and systems flowcharting symbols.

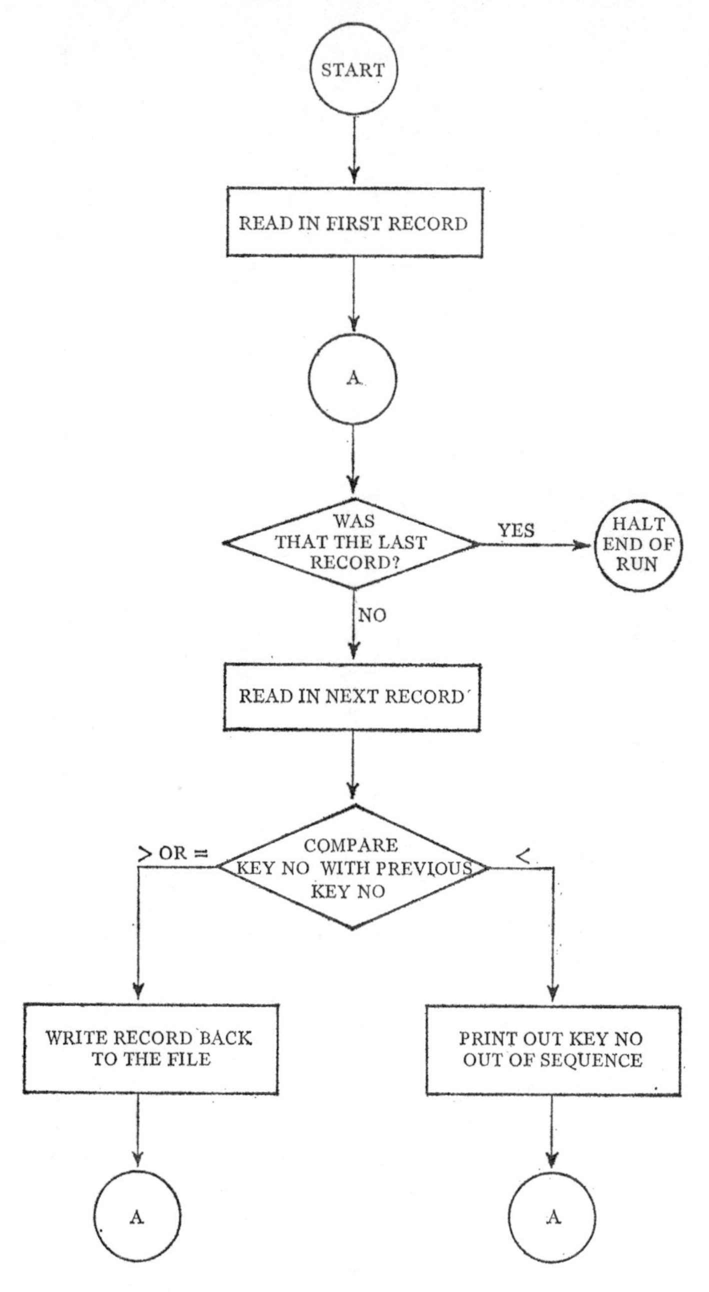

FIGURE 12 Simplified program flowchart to check the ascending sequence of a series of records.

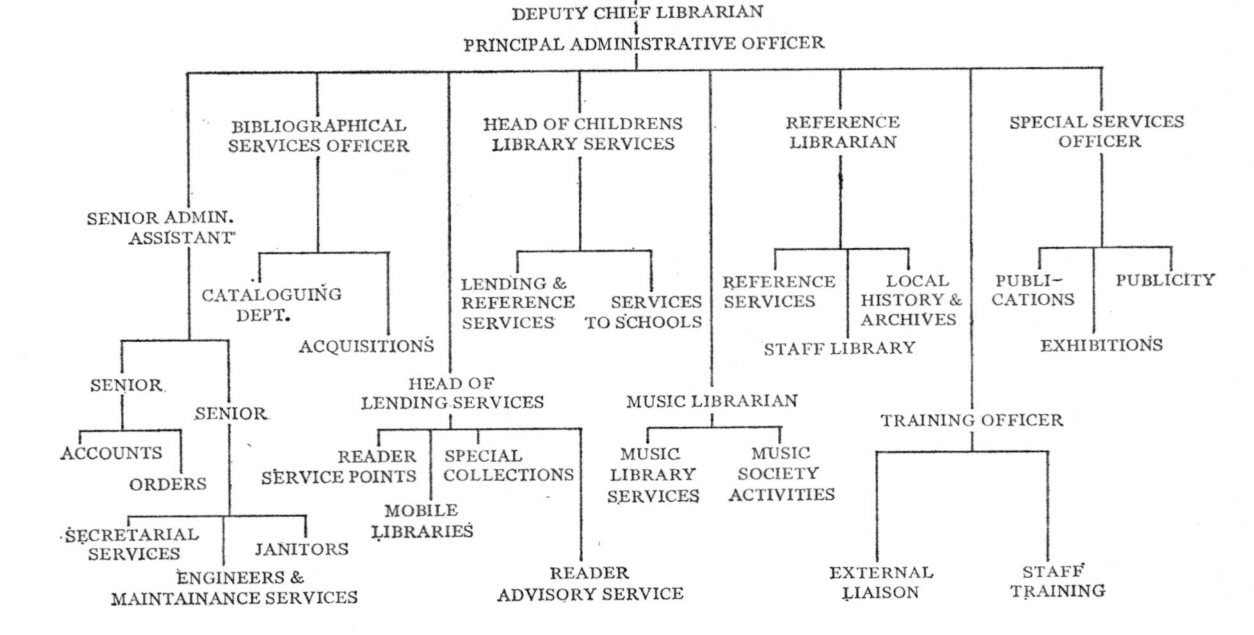

FIGURE 13 Organisation chart for a library system.

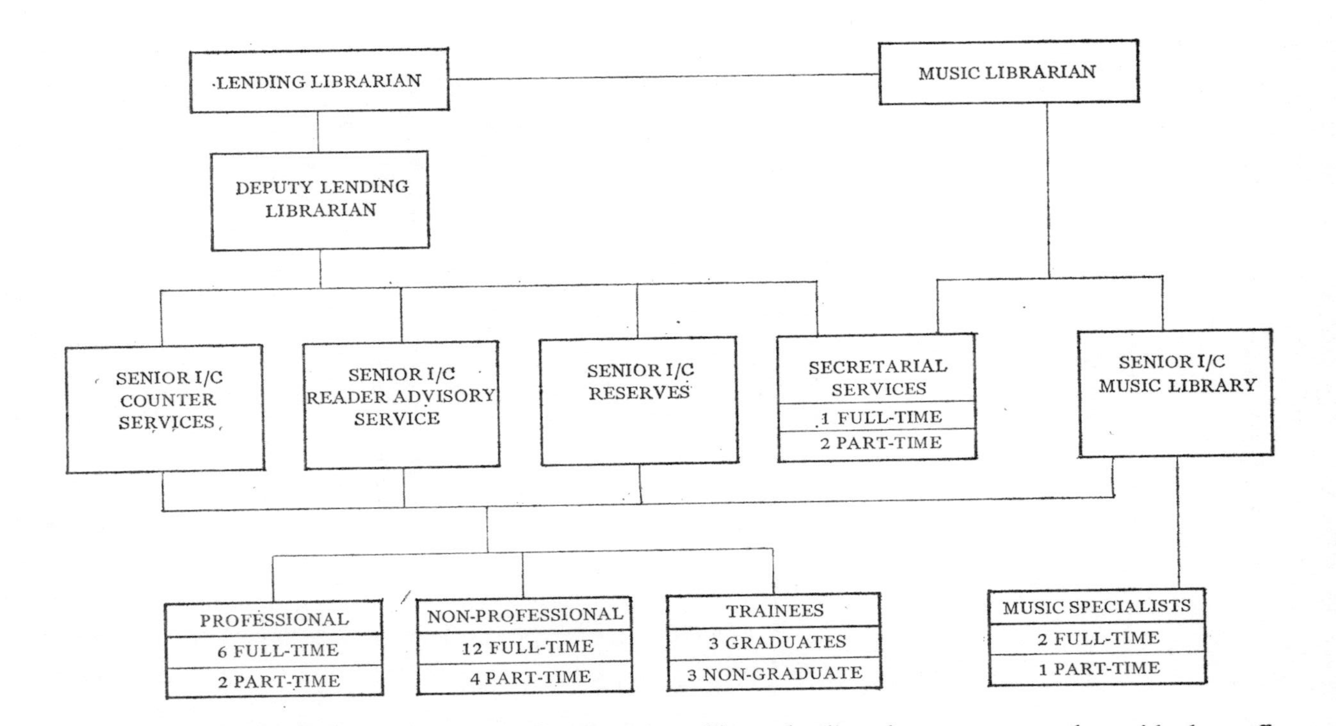

FIGURE 14 Outline chart showing the work sectors in a library lending department, together with the staff concerned.

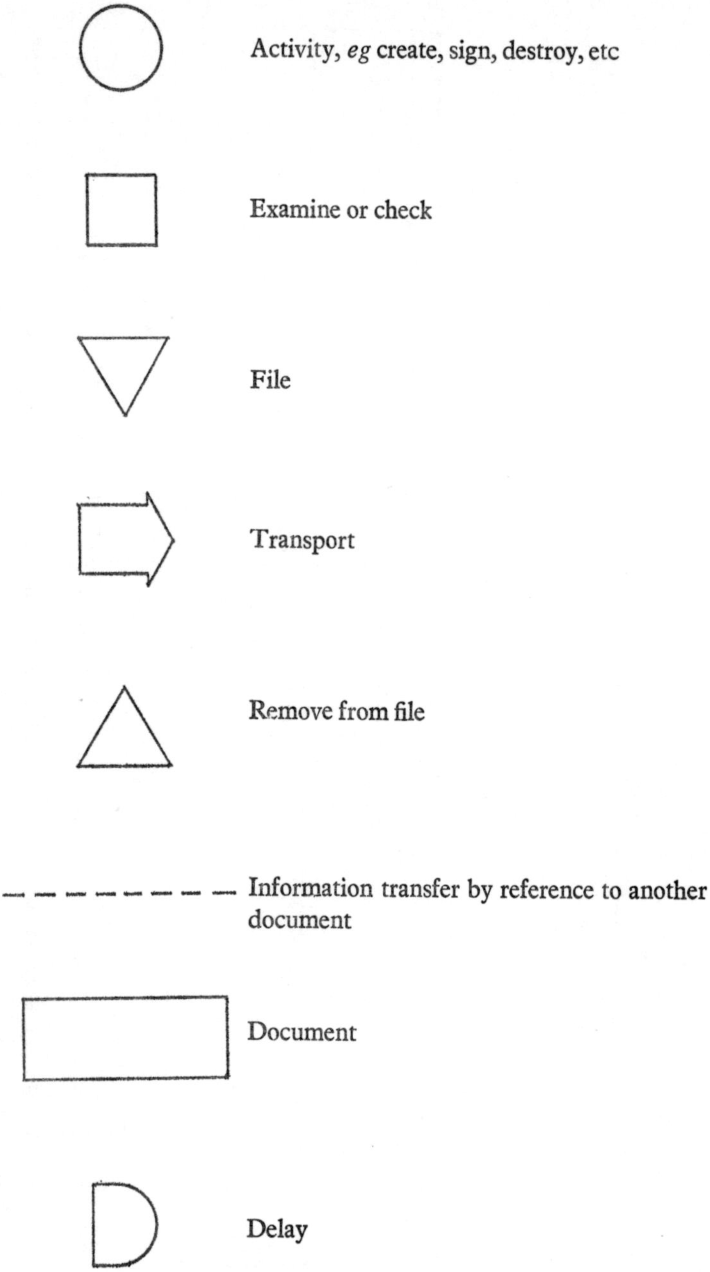

Activity, *eg* create, sign, destroy, etc

Examine or check

File

Transport

Remove from file

Information transfer by reference to another document

Document

Delay

FIGURE 15 Symbols used for process flowcharting.

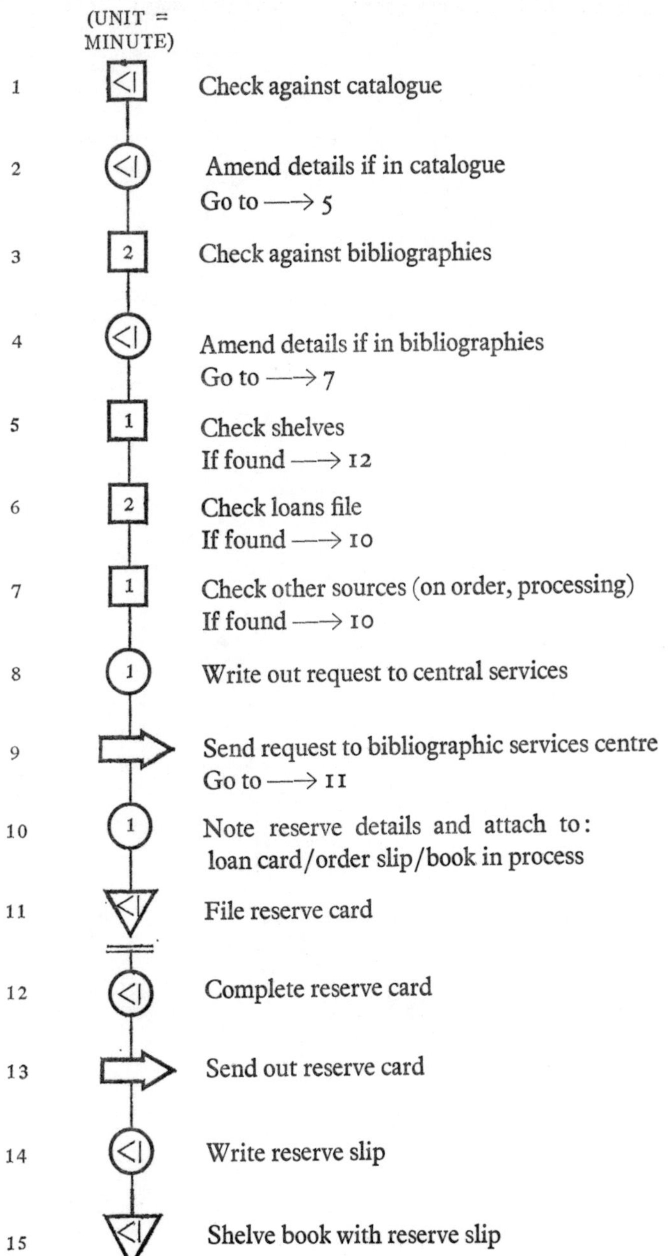

FIGURE 16 Linear record of a reservations procedure.

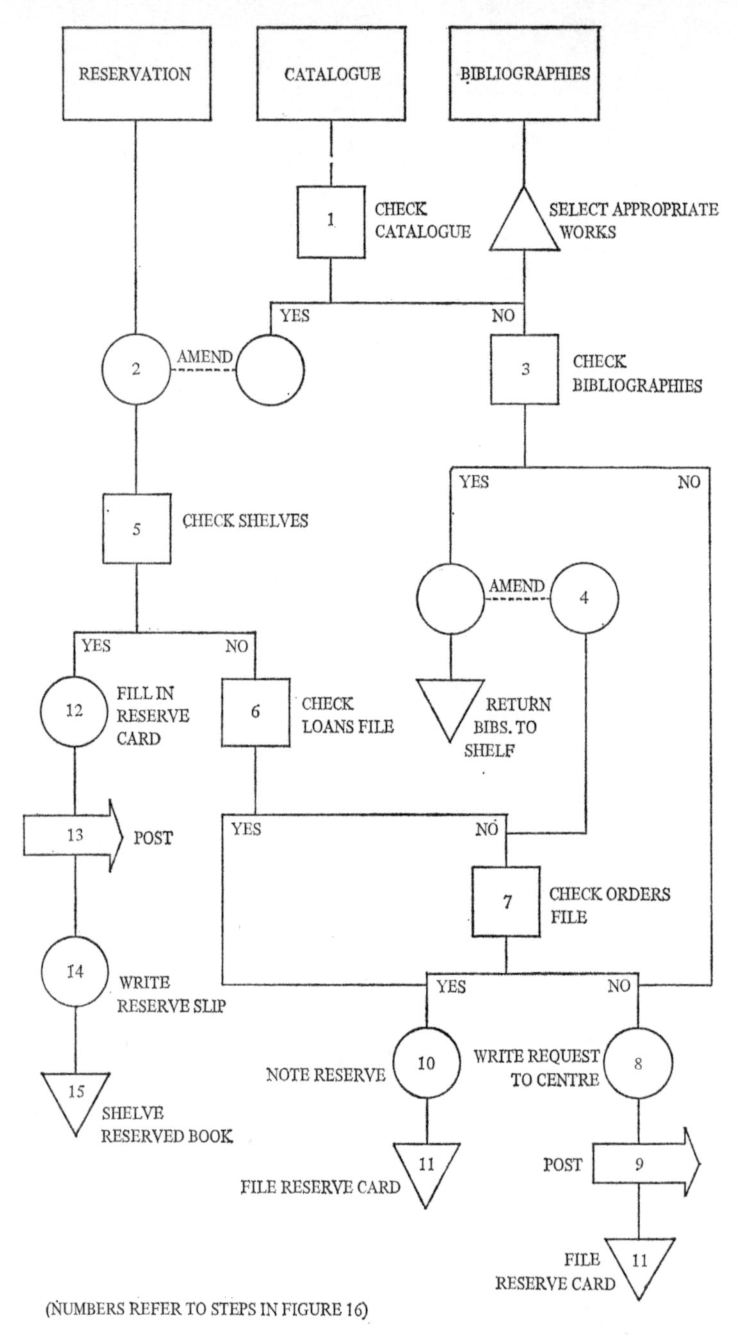

FIGURE 17 Process flowchart of a reservations procedure.

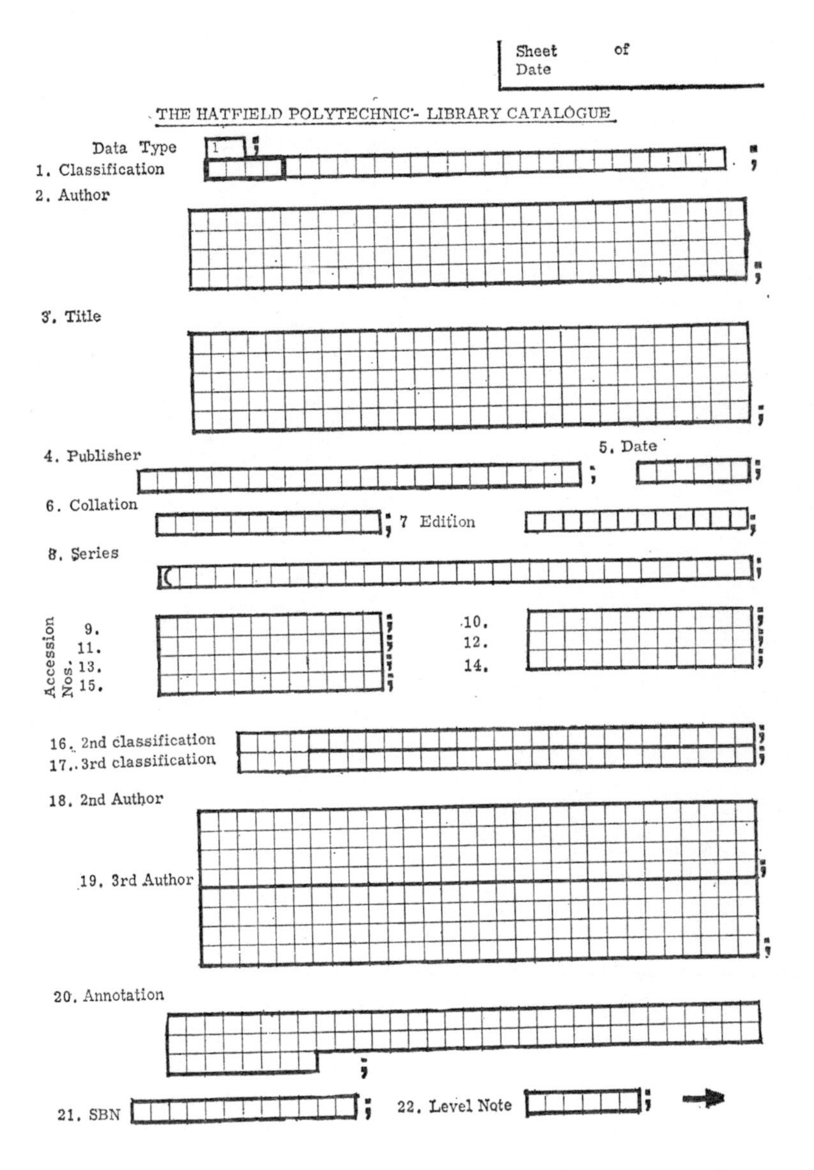
Sheet of
Date

THE HATFIELD POLYTECHNIC - LIBRARY CATALOGUE

Data Type 1 ;
1. Classification ;
2. Author ;
3. Title ;
4. Publisher ;
5. Date ;
6. Collation ;
7 Edition ;
8. Series ;
Accession Nos.
9. ;
10. ;
11. ;
12. ;
13. ;
14. ;
15. ;
16. 2nd classification ;
17. 3rd classification ;
18. 2nd Author ;
19. 3rd Author ;
20. Annotation ;
21. SBN ;
22. Level Note ;

FIGURE 18 Punching sheet for submitting a catalogue entry.
(Reproduced by kind permission of Hatfield Polytechnic Library, Herts)

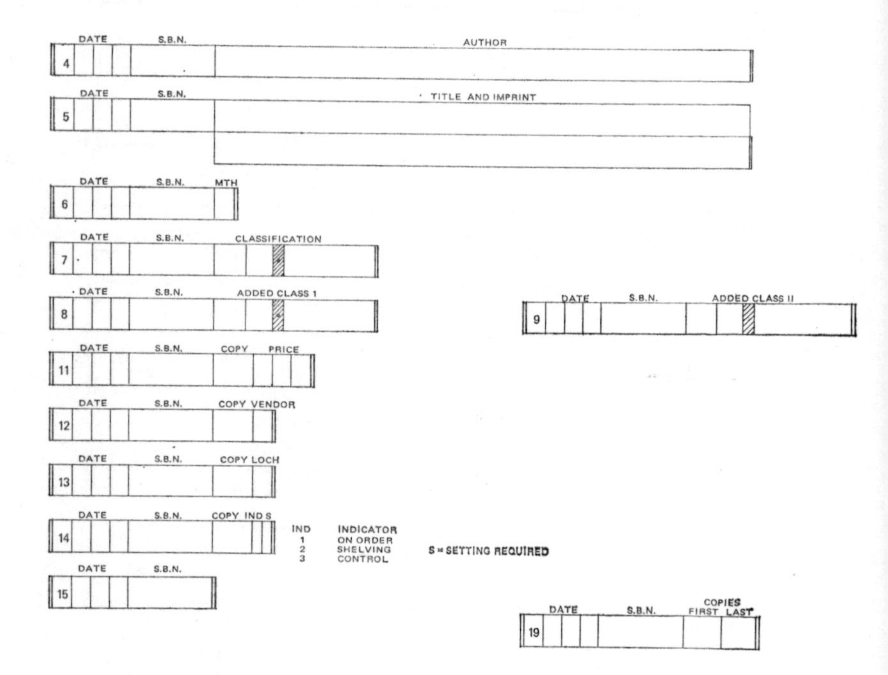
WESTMINSTER AND KENSINGTON & CHELSEA JOINT COMPUTER COMMITTEE
WESTMINSTER CITY LIBRARIES – CATALOGUE AMENDMENTS

4 DATE S.B.N. AUTHOR

5 DATE S.B.N. TITLE AND IMPRINT

6 DATE S.B.N. MTH

7 DATE S.B.N. CLASSIFICATION

8 DATE S.B.N. ADDED CLASS 1

9 DATE S.B.N. ADDED CLASS II

11 DATE S.B.N. COPY PRICE

12 DATE S.B.N. COPY VENDOR

13 DATE S.B.N. COPY LOCH

14 DATE S.B.N. COPY IND S

IND	INDICATOR
1	ON ORDER
2	SHELVING
3	CONTROL

S = SETTING REQUIRED

15 DATE S.B.N.

19 DATE S.B.N. COPIES FIRST LAST

FIGURE 19 Punching sheet for submitting corrections.
(Reproduced by kind permission of Westminster City Libraries)

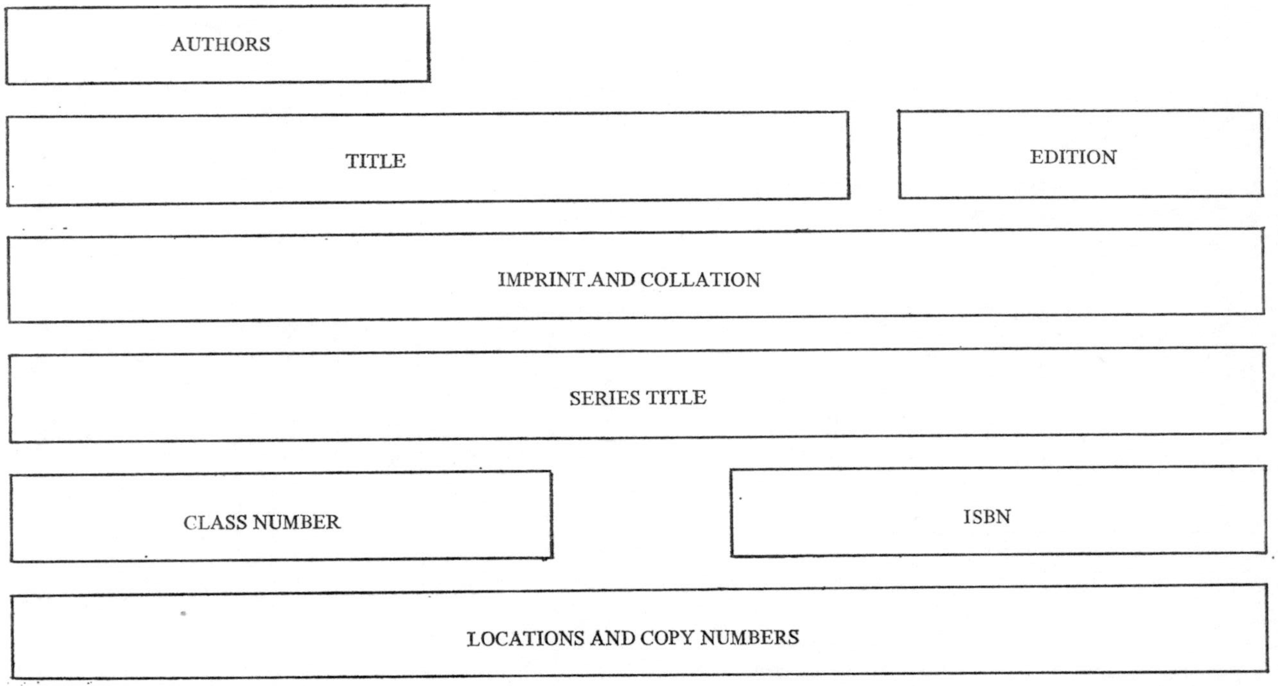

AUTHORS

TITLE EDITION

IMPRINT AND COLLATION

SERIES TITLE

CLASS NUMBER ISBN

LOCATIONS AND COPY NUMBERS

FIGURE 20 Useful data elements in a bibliographic record.

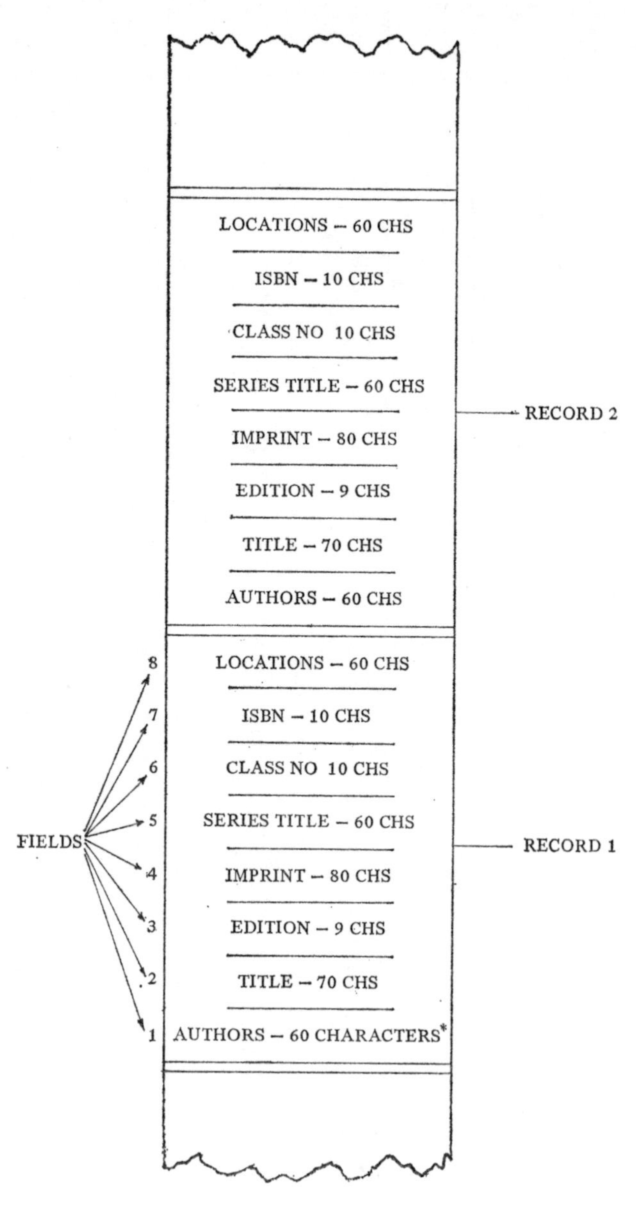

FIGURE 21 Data elements presented in fixed field format.

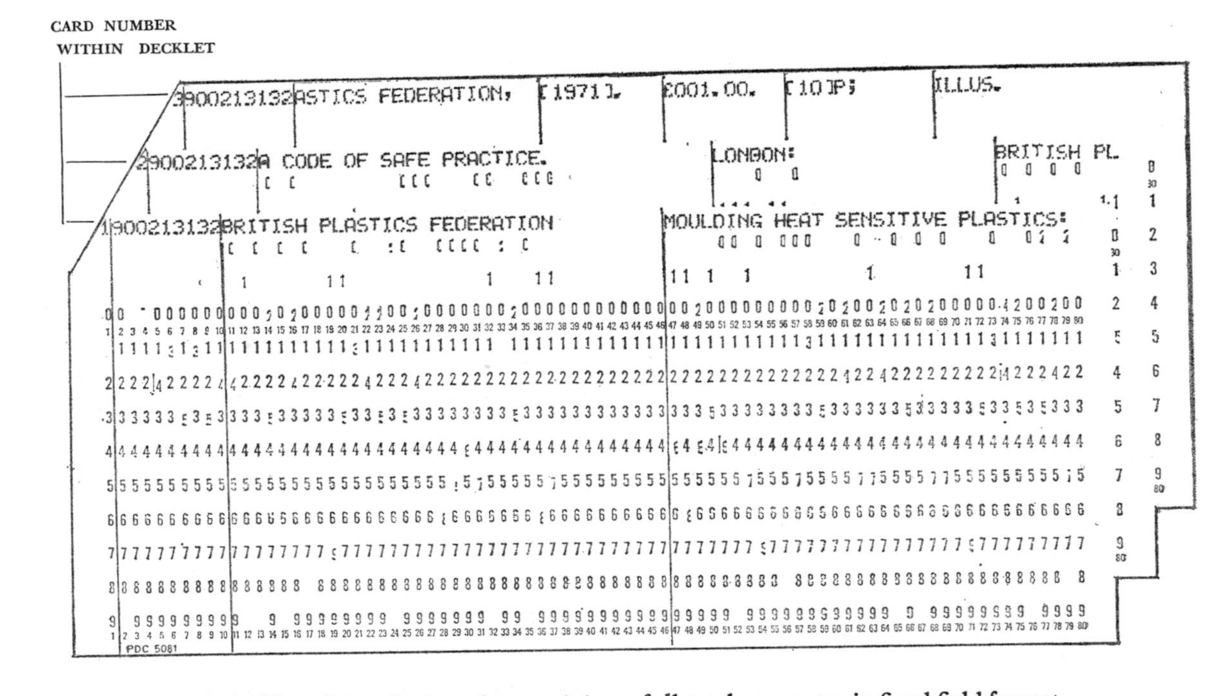

FIGURE 22 A decklet of punched cards containing a full catalogue entry in fixed field format.

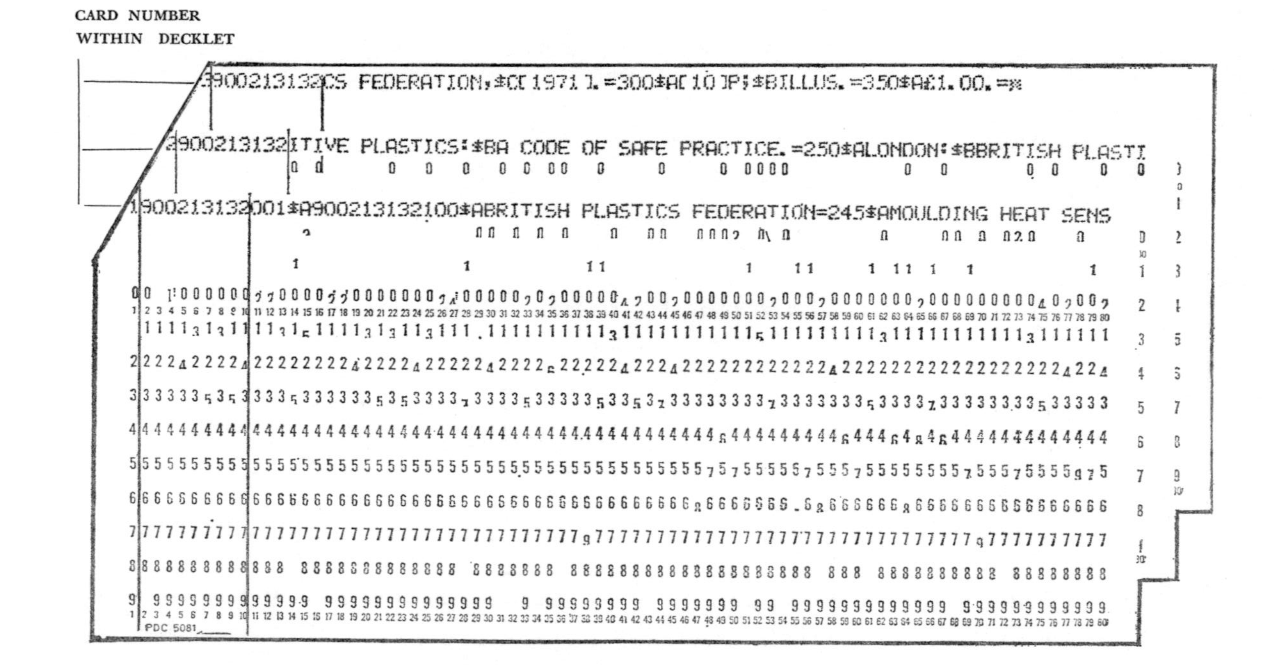

FIGURE 23 A similar set of cards having the data in variable field format, showing the tags preceding each field.

REVISED LIST OF MARC II TAGS

CONTROL FIELDS
0 0 1 Control Number
0 0 2 Sub-Record Directory
0 0 3 Reserved
0 0 4 Cataloging Source
0 0 8 Fixed Fields
0 0 9 Languages

CONTROL NUMBERS
0 1 0 LC Card Number
0 1 1 Linking LC Card Number
0 1 5 National Bibliography Number
0 1 6 Linking NBN
0 2 0 Standard Book Number
0 2 1 Linking SBN
0 2 5 Overseas Acquisitions Number (PL480, LACAP, etc.)
0 2 6 Linking OAN Number
0 3 5 Local System Number
0 3 6 Linking Local Number
0 3 9 Search Code

KNOWLEDGE NUMBERS
0 5 0 LC Call Number
0 5 1 Copy Statement
0 6 0 NLM Call Number
0 7 0 NAL Call Number
0 7 1 NAL Subject Category Number
0 8 0 UDC Number
0 8 1 BNB Classification Number
0 8 2 Dewey Decimal Classification No.
0 9 0 Local Call Number

MAIN ENTRY
1 0 0 Personal Name
1 1 0 Corporate Name
1 1 1 Conference or Meeting
1 3 0 Uniform Title Heading

SUPPLIED TITLES
2 4 0 Uniform Title
2 4 1 Romanized Title
2 4 2 Translated Title
2 4 3 Uniform Title (Collective works) (Reserved for British MARC)

TITLE PARAGRAPH
2 4 5 Title
2 5 0 Edition Statement
2 6 0 Imprint

COLLATION
3 0 0 Collation
3 5 0 Bibliographic Price
3 6 0 Converted Price

SERIES NOTES
4 0 0 Personal Name-Title (Traced Same)
4 1 0 Corporate Name-Title (Traced Same)
4 1 1 Conference-Title (Traced Same)
4 4 0 Title (Traced Same)
4 9 0 Series Untraced or Traced Differently

BIBLIOGRAPHIC NOTES
5 0 0 General Notes
5 0 1 "Bound with" Note
5 0 2 Dissertation Note
5 0 3 Bibliographic history Note
5 0 4 Bibliography Note
5 0 5 Contents Note (Formatted)
5 0 6 "Limited use" Note
5 2 0 Abstract

SUBJECT ADDED ENTRY
6 0 0 Personal Name
6 1 0 Corporate Name (excluding political jurisdiction alone)
6 1 1 Conference or Meeting
6 3 0 Uniform Title Heading

LC Subject Headings
6 5 0 Topical
6 5 1 Geographic Names
6 5 2 Political Jurisdiction Alone or with Subject Subdivisions
6 5 3 Proper Names Not Capable of Authorship
6 5 4 Headings Modified for Children

Other Subject Headings
6 6 0 NLM Subject Headings (MESH)
6 7 0 NAL Subject Headings (Agricultural/Biological Vocabulary)
6 9 0 Local Subject Heading Systems

OTHER ADDED ENTRIES
7 0 0 Personal Name
7 1 0 Corporate Name
7 1 1 Conference or Meeting
7 3 0 Uniform Title Heading
7 4 0 Title Traced Differently
7 5 3 Proper Name Not Capable of Authorship

SERIES ADDED ENTRIES
8 0 0 Personal Name-Title
8 1 0 Corporate Name-Title
8 1 1 Conference or Meeting-Title
8 4 0 Title

9 0 0 BLOCK OF 100 NUMBERS FOR LOCAL USE

FIGURE 24 Field tags used for the MARC II format.

Leader   Record Directory

00731 | N | A | M | b̸b̸ | 2 | 2 | 00181 | b̸b̸b̸b̸b̸b̸+001001100000 | 008

004100011 | 081001400052 | 082001200066 | 111009200078

245016900170 | 260005300339 | 300002400392 | 350000900416

650005600425 | 700001600481 | 700001800497 | 710003500515+

Control Fields (fixed fields)
Control No. (SBN)   Information Codes

0901740098+ | | 690903 | S | 1969 | b̸b̸b̸b̸ | EN | b̸b̸b̸b̸b̸b̸

Data (variable fields)

b̸b̸b̸b̸ | 01001 | b̸b̸ | ENG | b̸b̸b̸ | 00£A | 331.152AD+ | 00£A | 331.152+

00£A | NATIONAL CONFERENCE ON WORKERS' CONTROL AND

INDUSTRIAL DEMOCRACY | £M | 6TH £L NOTTINGHAM | £K | 1968+

10£A | HOW AND WHY INDUSTRY MUST BE DEMOCRATISED

£B | PAPERS SUBMITTED TO THE WORKERS' CONTROL CONFERENCE

(NOTTINGHAM, MARCH 30-31ST 1968) | £C EDITED BY KEN COATES

& WYN WILLIAMS+00£A | NOTTINGHAM | £B | INSTITUTE FOR WORKERS'

CONTROL | £C | 1969+ | etc.

FIGURE 25 A MARC record as it might appear on magnetic tape.

PE

PERIODICAL TITLES—ALPHABETICAL BY TITLE

Title	CODEN
PENNSYLVANIA C P A SPOKESMAN /CERTIFIED PUBLIC ACCOUNTANT/	PNSP-A
PENNSYLVANIA DENTAL JOURNAL, PENNSYLVANIA DENTAL SOCIETY	PEDJ-A
PENNSYLVANIA DENTAL SOCIETY, PENNSYLVANIA DENTAL JOURNAL	PEDJ-A
PENNSYLVANIA, DEPARTMENT OF AGRICULTURE, BULLETIN	PAGB-A
PENNSYLVANIA, DEPARTMENT OF FORESTS AND WATERS, PUBLICATIONS	PDWP-A
PENNSYLVANIA, DEPARTMENT OF INTERNAL AFFAIRS, MONTHLY BULLETIN	PDAB-A
PENNSYLVANIA FARMER	PENF-A
PENNSYLVANIA FORESTS	PAFO-A
PENNSYLVANIA FRUIT NEWS	PAFN-A
PENNSYLVANIA GAME NEWS	PAGN-A
PENNSYLVANIA MEDICAL JOURNAL	PMJO-A
PENNSYLVANIA PHARMACIST	PNPH-A
PENNSYLVANIA RETAIL FLORISTS, BULLETIN	PRFB-A
PENNSYLVANIA STATE ASSOCIATION OF MUTUAL INSURANCE COMPANIES, MUTUAL INSURANCE JOURNAL-NEWS	MIJN-A
PENNSYLVANIA STATE FOREST SCHOOL, RESEARCH PAPER	PSFP-A
PENNSYLVANIA STATE UNIVERSITY, AGRICULTURAL EXPERIMENT STATION, BULLETIN	PAAB-A
PENNSYLVANIA STATE UNIVERSITY, AGRICULTURAL EXPERIMENT STATION, PROGRESS REPORT	PAAR-A
PENNSYLVANIA UNIVERSITY, MORRIS ABORETUM, ABORETUM BULLETIN OF THE ASSOCIATES	ABAA-A
PENNSYLVANIA UNIVERSITY, PENN DENTAL JOURNAL	PNDJ-A
PENNSYLVANIA UNIVERSITY, UNIVERSITY MUSEUM BULLETIN	UKBP-A
PENNSYLVANIA UNIVERSITY, VETERINARY EXTENSION QUARTERLY	UPVQ-A
PENNSYLVANIA WATER WORK OPERATORS ASSOCIATION, JOURNAL	JPEW-A
PENROSE ANNUAL	PENA-A
PENSEZ PLASTIQUES	PEPL-A
PENZENSKII GOSUDARSTVENNYI PEDAGOGICHESKII INSTITUT, UCHENYE ZAPISKI	UPGP-A
PENZENSKII SEL/SKOKHOZYAISTVENNYI INSTITUT, SBORNIK STUDENCHESKIKH NAUCHNYKH RABOT	SNPI-A
PENZENSKII SEL/SKOKHOZYAISTVENNYI INSTITUT, SBORNIK TRUDOV	SPSI-A
PENZENSKII SEL/SKOKHOZYAISTVENNYI INSTITUT, TRUDY	TPSI-A
PENZENSKII SEL/SKOKHOZYAISTVENNYI INSTITUT, UCHENYE ZAPISKI	UPSI-A
PEORIA MILK PRODUCERS IN WHITLOCK. MILK PRODUCER	MLKP-A
PEPTIDES. PROCEEDINGS OF THE EUROPEAN SYMPOSIUM	PPES-A
PERADENIYA MANUAL /CEYLON/	PDYM-A
PERCEPTUAL AND MOTOR SKILLS	PMOS-A
PERCY FITZPATRICK INSTITUTE OF AFRICAN ORNITHOLOGY, SOUTH AFRICAN AVIFAUNA SERIES	SAFO-A

FIGURE 26 The 5-character abbreviations for periodical titles (CODEN) as devised by the American Society for Testing and Materials.

```
00771NAM  2200217       0010011000000080041000110500013000520810014000650820011000792400030000902450
1950012025000110031526000530032630000250037935000080040444000400041250300340045265200250048670000260
05117100C1700537 0901275042 690917S1968    EN A          00001  ENG   00$ADA690.N8 00$A942.55 1' 00$A
942.55 14$ATHE NORTHAMPTON SHOEMAKER 11$A'SNOBOPOLIS'$BNORTHAMPTON IN 1869:  'THE NORTHAMPTON SHOEMA
KER'$CAN ARTICLE PUBLISHED IN 1869 IN THE MAGAZINE 'GOOD WORDS' AND HERE REPRINTED WITH ADDITIONAL I
NFORMATION BY VICTOR A. HATLEY' 00$A2ND ED 00$ANORTHAMPTON$BNORTHAMPTON HISTORICAL SERIES$C1968 00$A
8P$B3ILLUS$C25CM$ESD 00$A2/6 10$ANORTHAMPTON HISTORICAL SERIES$VNO.1 00$APREVIOUS ED. (B67-16123) 19
66 00$ANORTHAMPTON$UHISTORY 11$AHATLEY$HVICTOR ARTHUR 21$A'GOOD WORDS'*

00729NAM  2200193       0010011000000080041000110810023000520820026000751000026001012450118001272500
0110024526000530025630000330030935000080034244000400035050300340039065000470042465000650047 1 0901275
050 690917S1968    EN AH       00001  ENG   00$A331.3885312D255 1' 00$A331.38$B8531$C0074255 10$AHA
TLEY$HVICTOR ARTHUR 14$ATHE ST GILES' SHOE-SCHOOL$BAN INCIDENT IN THE HISTORY OF SHOE MANUFACTURING
AT NORTHAMPTON$C BY VICTOR A. HATLEY' 00$A2ND ED 00$ANORTHAMPTON$BNORTHAMPTON HISTORICAL SERIES$C196
8 00$A7P$B2ILLUS, FACSIM$C25CM$ESD 00$A2/6 10$ANORTHAMPTON HISTORICAL SERIES$VNO.4 00$APREVIOUS ED.
(B67-15612) 1966 00$ACHILDREN$WEMPLOYMENT$VNORTHAMPTON$UHISTORY 00$ABOOTS AND SHOES$WTRADE AND MANUF
ACTURES$VNORTHAMPTON$UHISTORY*

00707NAM  2200181       0010011000000080041000110810015000520820018000671000017000852450125001022600
0550022730000170028235000080029944000400030750301160034765200370046370000260050 0 0901275069 690917S1
969    EN          00001  ENG   00$A324.42 S74 00$A324.2$C094255 10$AROWELL$HJOHN 14$ATHE NORTHAMPT
ON ELECTION OF 1774$BAN EYE-WITNESS ACCOUNT$C BY JOHN ROWELL; EDITED WITH A COMMENTARY BY VICTOR A.
HATLEY' 00$ANORTHAMPTON$BNORTHAMPTON HISTORICAL SERIES$C 1969' 00$A8P$C25CM$ESD 00$A2/6 10$ANORTHAMP
TON HISTORICAL SERIES$VNO.5 00$A'REPRINTED (WITH REVISIONS) FROM THE "REPORTS & PAPERS OF THE NORTHA
MPTONSHIRE ANTIQUARIAN SOCIETY" 1958 & 1959 00$AGT. BRIT.$WPARLIAMENT$WELECTIONS 11$AHATLEY$HVICTOR
ARTHUR*
```

FIGURE 27 A dump printout of a MARC record.

CLASS No.	AUTHOR AND TITLE
636.71 POODLE	HOPKINS, LYDIA NEW COMPLETE POODLE. HOWELL, 5TH ED. 1969
615.1073	HOPKINS, SIDNEY JOHN PRINCIPAL DRUGS: AN ALPHABETICAL GUIDE. 3RD ED. FABER, 1969
791.913	HOPKINSON, PETER SPLIT FOCUS: AN INVOLVEMENT IN TWO DECADES. HART, 1969
711.558	HOPPER, HENRY THOMAS PROVISION AND MAINTENANCE OF PLAYING FIELDS AND CHURCHYARDS TRADE & TECHNICAL P.,1967
F 978	HORAN, JAMES D. AND SANN, PAUL PICTORIAL HISTORY OF THE WILD WEST. SPRING BKS.,
GE 833.HORBACH	HORBACH, MICHAEL TITANEN: ROMAN. JUNCKER, 1970
641.55	HORLEY, GEORGINA GOOD FOOD ON A BUDGET. PENGUIN, 1969
641.5	HORLEY, GEORGINA GOOD FOOD ON A BUDGET. DEUTSCH, 1970
940.4144	HORNE, ALISTAIR DEATH OF A GENERATION: FROM NEUVE CHAPELLE TO VERDUN AND THE SOMME. MACDONALD, 1970
942.085	HORNE, DONALD GOD IS AN ENGLISHMAN. ANGUS, 1970
	HORNSEY AND... HORNSEY AND DISTRICT LOCAL DIRECTORY, 1968-1969. KEMP, 1969
327.1	HOROWITZ, DAVID CONTAINMENT AND REVOLUTION. BLOND, 1967
794.1	HOROWITZ, ISRAEL ALBERT CHESS OPENINGS: THEORY AND PRACTICE. FABER, 1965
612.017	HORROBIN, DAVID FREDERICK PRINCIPLES OF BIOLOGICAL CONTROL. MTP, 1970
F 332.152	HORSEFIELD, JAMES KEITH INTERNATIONAL MONETARY FUND, 1945-1965. I.M.F., 1969. 3V.
032	HORSLEY, E.M. HUTCHINSON'S NEW 20TH CENTURY ENCYCLOPEDIA. 5TH ED. 1970
796.352	HORTON, TOMMY GOLF: THE SHORT GAME. BATSFORD, 1970
942.54T	HOSKINS, WILLIAM GEORGE LEICESTERSHIRE. FABER, 1970. (SHELL GUIDE)
647.95029	HOTEL, RESTAURANT... HOTEL, RESTAURANT & CANTEEN SUPPLIES. BUSINESS DICTIONARIES

FIGURE 28 Sample page from an author catalogue which has been printed out by a line printer in the usual way, and then reduced onto A4 size pages. Less than actual size.
(Reproduced by kind permission of Westminster City Libraries)

BRADBROOK, MAURIEL CLARA GA 25510

IBSEN, THE NORWEGIAN. A REVOLUTION. BY MURIEL CLARA
BRADBROOK.
LONDON: CHATTO AND WINDUS 1946. 10,150 S.
C18867

BRADY, GERARD KEVIN GA 23571

SAINT DOMINIC. PILGRIM OF LIGHT. BY GERARD KEVIN
BRADY. WITH A PREFACE BY CARDINAL LERCARO.
LONDON: BURNS AND OATES 1957. 17,169 S.
G21025

BRAND, JOHN CHARLES DRURY SB 3550

MOLECULAR STRUCTURE. THE PHYSICAL APPROACH. BY JOHN
CHARLES DRURY BRAND AND JAMES CLARE SPEAKMAN.
LONDON: ARNOLD 1960. 8,300 S.
G20720

BRAY, ROBERT STOW SB 3555

STUDIES ON THE EXO-ERYTHROCYTIC CYCLE IN THE GENUS
PLASMODIUM. BY ROBERT STOW BRAY.
LONDON: LEWIS 1957. 7,192 S.
(LONDON SCHOOL OF HYGIENE AND TROPICAL MEDICINE.
MEMOIR. 12.)
G21177

LONDON: CHURCHILL 1961. 12,454 S.
G21053

BROGAN, DENIS WILLIAM GB 30306

THE DEVELOPMENT OF MODERN FRANCE. 1870-1939. BY
DENIS WILLIAM BROGAN.
LONDON: HAMILTON 1949. 10,744 S.
C18868

BROME, VINCENT GB 30187

ANEURIN BEVAN. A BIOGRAPHY. VON VINCENT BROME.
LONDON USW.: LONGMANS, GREEN AND CO. 1953. 7,244 S.
C18104

BROOKE, ROSALIND BECKFORD GB 29399

EARLY FRANCISCAN GOVERNMENT. ELIAS TO BONAVENTURE.
BY ROSALIND BECKFORD BROOKE.
CAMBRIDGE: UNIV. PR. 1959. 15,313 S.
(CAMBRIDGE STUDIES IN MEDIEVAL LIFE AND THOUGHT.
N.S. 7.)
G21159

BROOKE, RUPERT GA 25693

DEMOCRACY AND THE ARTS. BY RUPERT BROOKE. WITH A
PREFACE BY GEOFFREY KEYNES.
LONDON: HART-DAVIS 1946. 8,32 S.
C18242

FIGURE 29 Sample page from the author catalogue of Bochum University. This illustration is a much reduced copy of the computer version.
(Reproduced by kind permission of the University Library)

bibliography

Suggestions for further reading:

Batty, C D *ed*: *Libraries and machines today*. Scunthorpe: North Midland Branch of the Library Association. First edition 1966 (56 pages), second edition 1967 (50 pages).

Bourne, C P: *Methods of information handling*. New York: Wiley, 1963. 241 pages.

Chandor, A *et al*: *Practical systems analysis*. London: Hart-Davies, 1969. 388 pages.

Coward, R E *ed*: *MARC record service proposals*. London: British National Bibliography, 1968. (BNB/MARC documentation service publication no 1.)

Cox, N S M *et al*: *The computer and the library*. University of Newcastle upon Tyne; Hamden (Connecticut): The Shoe String Press, 1966, 96 pages.

Cox, N S M and Grose, M W *eds*: *Organisation and handling of bibliographic records by computer*. London: Oriel Press; Hamden, (Connecticut): The Shoe String Press, 1967. 191 pages.

Daniels, A and Yeats, D *eds*: *Basic training in systems analysis*. London: Pitman/NCC, 1969. 275 pages.

Dolby, James L: 'An algorithm for variable length proper-name compression' in *Journal of library automation* 3(4), December 1970. Pages 257-275.

Dougherty, R M and Heinritz, F J: *Scientific management of library operations*. New York: Scarecrow Press, 1966.

Gilchrist, A: 'Further comment on the terminology of the analysis of library systems' in *Aslib proceedings* 20(10), October 1968. Pages 408-412.

Harrison, J and Laslett, P *eds*: *The Brasenose conference on the automation of libraries*. London: Mansel, 1967. 175 pages.

Harvey, J *ed*: *Data processing in public and university libraries*. London: Macmillan, 1966. 150 pages.

Hayes, R M and Becker, J: *Handbook of data processing for libraries*. New York: Becker and Hayes Inc, 1970. 885 pages.

Kimber, R: *Automation in libraries*. Oxford: Pergamon Press, 1968. 140 pages.

Laver, F J M: *Introducing computers*. London: HMSO, 1965. 69 pages.

Licklider, J C R: *Libraries of the future*. Massachusetts: MIT Press, 1965. 219 pages.

Mitchell, R K: *Information science and computer basics: an introduction*. London: Clive Bingley; Hamden (Connecticut): The Shoe String Press, 1971. 101 pages.

Phillips, A H: *Computer peripherals and typesetting*. London: HMSO, 1968. 665 pages.

Robinson, F *et al*: *Systems analysis in libraries*. London: Oriel Press.

Ruecking, F H: 'Bibliographic retrieval from bibliographic input' in *Journal of library automation* 1(4), December 1968. Pages 227-238.

Scientific American: *Information*. San Francisco: W H Freeman & Co, 1966. 218 pages.

Periodicals frequently carrying articles on computer applications in libraries:

Aslib proceedings. 1949-. (M) London: Aslib.

College and research libraries. 1939-. (BiM) American Library Association.

Journal of Documentation. 1927-. (Q). London: Aslib.

Journal of library automation. 1968-. (Q) American Library Association.

Library resources and technical services, 1957-. (Q) American Library Association.

Program. 1966-. (Q) London: Aslib.

index

This index has been compiled after the style of PRECIS developed by the British National Bibliography. The facet order for the main entries is ACTIVITY: THING: TYPE: ASPECT. All added entries are derived from the main entries in this manner:

Main entries — A:
B:C:D.

Added entries — 1. B:A
C:D.
2. C:B:A
D.
3. D. C:
B:A

Where a facet would present an unsought term if brought to the indexing position, it is missed out. Thus entries 1 and 3 might be given, but entry 2 omitted as an unnecessary entry term. The suffixes a, b & c indicate the upper, middle or lower part of the page.